About the Author

Hooshmand Badee (PhD) is an academic economist, writer, and researcher with over thirty years of teaching experience. Having lived in the world's poorest and wealthiest nations for more than four decades, he has witnessed first-hand the inequalities in people's standard of living. Such observations fuelled his passion for exploring the potential of a new and sustainable economic life for humans and the environment. He has demonstrated this in several published books, papers and talks at numerous international conferences. He believes that this starts by working closely with the grassroots population to put them at the centre of economic activities.

To my children:

Nawgole

Vesal

&

Sahba

&

*To all those who are working on
transforming our present economic condition
into more sensible, equitable, sustainable
and prosperous communities.*

Towards

A

Sustainable Economic Life

How do we get from our present
condition into more sensible, equitable,
sustainable, and prosperous communities?

Hooshmand Badee

Cover designed by Sam Goodwin

Table of Contents

Introduction

Can humanity face and fix the challenges of the 21st century and beyond? Are the things prepared for a smooth transition to a prosperous future for all? The view that social structures constantly changes is central to responding to these questions. The history of economics has shown that no single economic theory has always suited the whole world. Humanity has reached a level of maturity capable of facing and fixing contemporary challenges. Development expert Farzam Arbab maintains that economies with different logic are entirely possible, and the only choices open to us are not the capitalist and socialist modes of production, both of which are products of two and three hundred years in the history of the European people. A mature humanity can develop an economy with a new logic not based on greed or false precepts of absolute equality that allows reasonable freedom yet promotes and safeguards justice.

What is happening in our global economy today in the name of global financial crises is timely to be re-examined for both developed and developing countries. It is felt that there is a need to regulate, control and even restrict the present economic condition to reshape the future global economy. The current free-market economy is only fair to some people. The missing part is on transforming our present condition into more sensible, equitable, sustainable and prosperous communities. This requires a network of human values centred mainly on economic justice to eliminate imbalances in the global market.

Sustainability is a condition for the market to produce goods and services suitable for human health, environmental protection, and the next generation's well-being. The operation of such competition requires guidance and control, which must be done through both the private and public sectors. The best kind of competition is competition in cooperation.

The capacity to think globally has increased, especially among the younger generation with a worldwide consciousness of knowledge, attitudes and skills needed for the proper functioning of meaningful integration, a prerequisite for an effective transformation of the economy. The embryonic condition for relative hope, integration and unity is created. Nations increasingly realise that interdependency is a prerequisite for their future prosperity.

Therefore, the essential part of this book is to keep our thoughts optimistic. Positive thinking can help reduce the impact of current adversarial and negative challenges and focus on building upon strength for a successful transformation.

The views expressed are that humans have reached a level of intellectual capacity and, to some extent, spiritual and moral maturity to understand and design social, political and economic models that are suitable for creating a better world. A future without discrimination, inequality, poverty, corruption and hatred. A positive view from the present to the future.

Chapter 1 -
Lessons learned from COVID-19

Introduction

Another external shock affected humanity; this time, it is COVID-19. According to the World Health Organisation (WHO), the estimated total number of global deaths attributed to the coronavirus Pandemic, with the latest deaths reported exceeding 3.3 million.

External shocks may happen at any time and are not predictable, and are not the same. They have a different impact on people and nature. They are sudden, unwelcome and mostly have ugly faces. These external shocks may affect our lives in many ways, depending on what kind of shocks we get. We have observed some of these shocks in the past, such as the bird-flu outbreak and mad cow disease, that started in one country and spread to other countries. It could be locally, nationally, and even globally. But, for some of us, the best example we have seen during our lifetime is COVID-19. Coronavirus is not local; it is not regional; it is global. It affected all nations at once, without discrimination. It put the economy globally in a loose, uncertain, unstable and risky situation.

Between 2019 and 2020, the number of people living in extreme poverty increased by an estimated fifty million and the resulting global economic downturn.[1]

Many people, including experts, were working on the idea that materialism, consumerism, the arms industry, and the sex industry may have a big part in destroying our communities. Still, we didn't think about an unimaginable horror like a virus has the power to do it. The most insignificant creature brought the most powerful nations in the world to their knees. The entire population has been affected and forced into isolation. Millions have lost their lives. Millions more have lost jobs, lowered income, and caused bankruptcy in many organisations, and government debts are rising. The whole sector of the economy was frozen. This was a sudden and unimaginable horror we experienced.

The two horrible parts of this virus are killing people and separating humans. Social distancing is the worst thing happening to us as humans. Touching, kissing, cuddling, walking, talking, and caring for each other are good parts of us that were missed by many. This is the moment that will be written in history. But the more critical factor that should be written is the lessons we learned from this. Today, humanity has some ideas about why we are in this condition and what we are learning from this Pandemic. There is so much information available to us and so many concerns. One important lesson for governments is to invest more in public health. A critical task for humans is to have a new way of thinking about the purpose of life and perhaps adapt ourselves to a new lifestyle.

Challenges

Although we want to be optimistic about a sensible and sustainable transition[2] to a better future, we should not be too naïve. With the current Pandemic, there are many challenges now, and they may continue in the future. For example, what is done or will be done for millions of refugees living in densely populated areas with deplorable conditions and minimal or no medical care access? What about one billion that are people living in absolute poverty without medical care and vaccination? Several gaps must be filled, including education, equal opportunity, productivity, wealth, resource allocation, and digital gap. These and many other challenges require immediate attention to reduce the risk of future Pandemics. Therefore, there is a need for restructuring the entire society, our hospitals, our educational institutions, our agriculture, our politics, our economics, and the way we live and our minds. The rights of people must be protected, especially those in the minority, the rights of women, the rights of ethnic and religious minorities, the rights of children, the rights of disabled people, and the rights of poor people. We are now sure that globalisation is a fact, and whether we want it or not, it will happen. A sensible and sustainable transition to purposeful globalisation requires a proper and strong foundation so that all enjoy the relative well-being, happiness and prosperity possible.

The challenging role of government during COVID-19 was a matter of concern for all communities. The paradox is about the role of government and the role of the market in free-market capitalism. One of the principal features of the free-market economy of capitalism, stated by its founders, is that the government should have no influential control and involvement in the market. At best, the government should have minimum participation in the market and economic activities. The market should be free to decide what is suitable for the participants. The view is that market actors are rational thinkers, and the market reaches equilibrium by itself. The instrument of invisible hands, which includes price system and competition, influences the decision-making of actors in the market to create a balanced economy. The paradox during COVID-19 was that the government expected the market to have strong participation in its eradication, and the market expected the government to step in and do its function. We saw many instances of a need for more cooperation and collaboration between these institutions of society.

However, today the notion is that COVID-19 and other external shocks, such as the 2008 global financial crisis, will expose some of the flaws of this thinking about the role of government and a free-market economy. If the main motive of a capitalist is profit maximisation, numerous activities in a society, such as various Pandemics, do not generate profit on their own. Therefore, active government intervention was needed and most urgently. As we saw, COVID-19 required all governments to respond with a large scale and intensity because the world was in a critical state. The virus was rapidly spreading across countries, requiring an army to fight against the spread of the Pandemic. On the one hand, governments must step in and inject financial stimulus packages into the economy, and on the other hand, try to slow the spread of the disease to protect vulnerable populations. By definition and in a free-market economy based on profit intensive, these activities are not those a capitalist is interested in.

The challenge, however, was that as the Pandemic happened suddenly, many governments were not properly prepared and equipped to deal effectively with such a catastrophe. These are a few examples: the absence of necessary and sufficient resources, shortage of human resources expertise, short-termism, politicising decision-making, etc. The result has made public-sector institutions ineffective when we need them to overcome crises like the COVID-19 Pandemic. We had similar situations, such as environmental damage, financial problems and external shocks. So, there is a government failure because there is too much emphasis on the free-market economy to fix the crises. As we noticed, the free-market economy is also failing because there was too much expectation that government should come forward and take care of the problem.

Opportunities

This is the message of people of the world frequently repeated on the news during this Pandemic, 'At this moment, we feel more united wherever we live than ever before, even at a distance.' The truth of the unity of humankind is becoming apparent to larger and larger numbers of people.

The recent development caused by COVID-19 is evidence that the functioning of traditional capitalism is in transition. This is a transformation process from self-interest to collective interest, from competition to solidarity and cooperation, and from the minimum involvement of government to high government participation for controlling and regulating the market.

On the one hand, governments must step in and inject financial stimulus packages into the economy. On the other hand, we are trying to slow the spread of the disease to protect vulnerable populations. By definition, and in a profit-intensive free-market economy, these are not the kind of activities that a capitalist is interested in. Also, as there was too much emphasis on the market to care for the economy, we noticed that governments were not adequately prepared and equipped to deal with a crisis such as COVID-19. Therefore, the current Pandemic is an opportunity to re-think our economy concerning government involvement and business models.

There are clear views that support government intervention in the market to balance the economy and advance a more equitable society, which also benefits the market. In particular, government involvement is required in those areas that the free-market economy does not show interest because there is little or no profit available. Hence, a government with the right plans and adequate resources can control and regulate the economy. Below, this chief responsibility is discussed further.

There was a reasonable collaboration between the two sectors of business organisations and government institutions. COVID-19 was an opportunity to re-think our economy about government involvement and business models. The approach will shift the focus to stimulating more sustainable economic growth by governments, and it will examine viable policy approaches to encourage the acceleration of socially and environmentally responsible business models.

It was encouraging to see that business organisations and governments were working together in response to the eradication of a Pandemic. It shows that collectively we can do good things and praiseworthy activities. It shows that we have altruistic nature within us, not only at the individual level but also at the institutional and governmental levels. Hundreds of examples are there that businesses are doing service projects. Here are a few suggestions for the government to become more effective. One is that governments must invest in and create various institutions to deal with crises. Another suggestion is that governments better coordinate their research and development activities. And finally, governments need to structure public-private partnerships to ensure that citizens and the economy benefit. Such activities make the transition smooth and operational and, at the same time, sensible and sustainable.

Apart from the unimaginable horror that humanity was going through during the recent Pandemic, opportunities are created for reflection. A whole new model of life will be made in all parts of our society, including hospitals, educational institutions, agriculture, banking, and Internet businesses. The kind of innovation that improves people's lives, a sustainable lifestyle, the innovation that improves people's lives with a balanced consumption and moderate lifestyle without damaging the environment.

The current Pandemic signalled that we must see the entire world as one unit, as one body. Therefore, the type of life we will have during the transition must consider the interdependence of all people and nations. This Pandemic has created an opportunity to identify the difficulties and challenges we may face at private and public institutions. The notion of self-interest has given way to collective interest, cooperation, and solidarity instead of aggressive competition. This shows that when people face difficulties, they can demonstrate unselfish and altruistic nature to some extent. Of course, we should not be too optimistic about this because some people missed the old days of materialistic life.

On the economic side, COVID-19 created opportunities, as many businesses started to operate locally, including the use of local currencies that, in recent times, have become less popular. This led to decreasing the strength of some of the more popular currencies. Strengthening local currencies expands economic activities at the local and regional levels. This is important because it increased the opportunity for many smaller and underdeveloped nations to trade with each other at the local and regional levels. Also, with better and stronger money, purchasing more advanced technology for economic development in areas such as increasing and improving agricultural products, advancing local manufacturing products, and expanding and advancing infrastructure is possible. In rural areas, people will be at the centre of economic activities. And it is essential to note that there are more cooperation and interconnectedness among people and businesses at the local level. This means other resources, such as natural and economic resources, will be used more efficiently and effectively. A whole new life model will be created in all parts of our society, including hospitals, educational institutions, agriculture, banking, business, the Internet, and online businesses. All these will improve living standards in the world's underdeveloped regions.

Therefore, one of the consequences of COVID-19 is the realisation of capitalism's excessive power and influence to control economic activities worldwide. One outcome of the Pandemic is lower demand in Europe and the United States and the effect of the high level of unemployment. This has caused many multinational corporations to stop functioning or operating part-time. Once again, we see that economic activities are increased locally. Opportunities are created for local businesses to respond to local needs. Such development has many advantages, including producing products demanded locally and using local resources. This will lead to increased employment opportunities and a higher standard of living for the grassroots population. Also, new opportunities are created in rural areas to develop new life models based on bottom-up rather than top-down planning. Increasing economic activities in rural areas may reduce the population in metropolitan cities and hence decrease many related problems in big cities, such as traffic congestion, pollution of all kinds, and much more.

Optimism for a brighter horizon

COVID-19 can be used to convince us that the interdependence of the peoples and nations of the world is a fact that no one can deny. These views reinforce the transition period to a sustainable and prosperous future. This message from the world's people was repeated frequently during this Pandemic in the media:

- The truth of the cooperation and interconnectedness of humankind is becoming apparent to more numbers of people.

- People and institutions are connected and coordinate responses to ensure that measures introduced by one group or nation do not hamper the reaction of others.

- This is a process for humanity to think and act together for the common good, a method of transformation from self-interest to collective interest.

- The dream of becoming connected is becoming a reality.

- At the level of business organisations, new ideas are shaping and reshaping, including: from profit-orientated objectives to service-orientated objectives; from hierarchies to team-working; from control to empowerment; from privacy to transparency; from dictatorial decision-making to consultative decision-making; and from competition to cooperation.

Conclusion

During COVID-19, many people were interested in knowing when life would return to normal. Or can we go back to business as usual? But what kind of life did we have before the Pandemic that many of us are interested in going back to it? What kind of normal life did many of us have? Poverty, hardship, hunger, deprivation, homelessness, extremes of wealth and poverty, and environmental degradation do not represent a sensible and sustainable normal life. Therefore, we don't want our life to return to the same normal but to a better life, to a more sustainable everyday life. We also should remember that this is a rehearsal period, practising to create an ideal lifestyle. And, of course, we should not expect that during a trial, everything goes perfectly. Mistakes happen as well.

Chapter 2 -
Avoiding future pandemics

Introduction

Sustainability, or sustainable development, is modern thinking with a dynamic concept. Sustainable development has a close and strong relationship between social, political, environmental, and virtuous elements necessary for a sensible and equitable economic transition. Economic sustainability creates a sense of balance in the market maintained over time. As a dynamic system, economic sustainability is discussed in life's social, political, and environmental aspects. Social sustainability in economics encompasses several areas, including the labour market, equal opportunity, governance, human rights, human advancement, security, and well-being. Environmental sustainability in economics is to attain a sustainable lifestyle by attempting to be careful about using the earth's resources to meet the current needs without upsetting nature and those of future generations. Virtuous sustainability in economics is the promotion of values at all market phases to impact participants' decision-making. Effective transition requires human responsibility and effective management to balance available resources that are needed for production, distribution and consumption.

The United Nations' standard definition of sustainable development states, "It is a development that meets the needs of the present without compromising the ability of future generations to meet their own needs."[3] Several indicators of sustainability at the market level are indicated in this statement, including the organisation of the market, the wise use of resources, coordination and development of the market, global equity, and the control of the market with regulations and restrictions.

Alternatively, economic sustainability is defined as 'the wise and just use of resources for producing goods and services that respond to basic human needs for attaining a sustainable lifestyle while protecting the Earth's resources.' This definition has built-in characteristics of sustainable production and consumption with consideration of distributive justice. It incorporates quality of life, the wise use of resources, including renewable resources within their capacity for renewal and global equity, along with justice in human actions and responsibilities towards the environment and the future generations that will come later. This is an onerous responsibility, doing and caring for those who do not exist currently. Thus, sustainability has an ethical component. This involves the exercise of justice and fairness in the sharing of resources between current and future generations.

With sustainability, human activities are closely linked to human values and moral incentives. For example, the view supports that our economy cannot be in isolation from nature. Sustainability, therefore, requires that the activities within the market be in harmony with the laws of nature.

Below, we continue the subject of sustainability with different phases of the production cycle, including needs and wants, organisation, production, the market, distribution, and consumption. Trustworthiness and truthfulness are keys to sustainability and successful operations at all market phases.

Stages of the cycle of production in a free-market economy

Our needs and wants

Needs and wants are the beginning of most economic activities. What motivates people and can lead to a change of behaviour are their needs and wants, which the individual and the broader social factors determine. Once the necessities are identified, a behaviour pattern will emerge to gratify them. When conflict arises between needs and wants, one's behaviour is affected. However, it should be noted that needs and wants to vary at different times in a person's life. Not all needs and wants are important for a person at any one time. People perceive necessities and luxuries differently at different times in their lives. These also depend on one's personality, level of income, type of employment, social environment and lifestyle. Essential commodities such as food, clothes and housing, and certain types of services such as health and education for physical and intellectual development are basic human rights and most fundamental. Economics is concerned with satisfying needs and wants. 'Wants' are created mainly by society. By changing society's value system, 'wants' could be modified, and the economic system transformed. This phase of economic sustainability aims to attain the most excellent satisfaction of needs and wants within the limits of moderation.

There is no set formula for human needs and wants. However, our needs and wants should be sensible, equitable and sustainable for an effective transition. They can be divided into essential and non-essential commodities. One of the most basic human needs is food, which in several cases is exploited by some food manufacturers who may not be concerned with nourishing people but with increasing profit. Shortage of sufficient food leads to malnutrition. At the same time, over-consumption of foodstuffs leads to severe problems such as addiction or obesity.

Business organisations

The success of an organisation is in producing commodities demanded by conscious consumers while simultaneously contemplating environmental protection with effective and efficient use of resources.

Implementing sustainability principles inspires consumers and producers to attain its objectives. The principles of equity and cooperation are helpful for 'needs', which are essential for living. For 'wants', which are non-essential, the principles of moderation and consultation are practical. The primary responsibility of producers is to establish a sustainable input-output process. This indicates that the degree of success and optimum level of sustainability depends on all stages of production, including the extraction of raw materials. Thus, this phase of economic sustainability aims to attain the most excellent satisfaction of needs and wants within the limits of moderation. In such an environment, consumer sovereignty is controlled, and utility maximisation is adjusted through making the right choices.

Production

Organisations have the function of production to satisfy human needs and wants by delivering goods and services that agree with the principle of sustainability. The primary responsibility should be towards social needs. They must use several guiding principles to channel an efficient and sustainable input-output process. The degree and optimum level of sustainability depend on all stages of production, including extraction of raw materials, conversion processes and the quality of the finished product.

Sustainability also requires products to be produced with attributes that fit the environment. The quality of goods and services depends on the resources available, including technology and skilled labour, and is also closely linked with attitudes towards work. This will ensure that everyone performs work with excellence in all stages of production, from carrying on research and development to producing the finished product. Such attitude towards work and the output level will control the over-production and under-production of specific goods and services that otherwise may defeat economic sustainability. Over-production or under-production is unsustainable; they are a reason for economic fluctuations, causing severe imbalances in the market due to the wastage of valuable and vulnerable 'rare earth' resources.

Sustainable production and capacity utilisation must go hand in hand. It should involve systems that enable households to participate and contribute towards advancing sustainability. Thus, the issue of participation in production is vital. The materially poor must participate directly in efforts to improve their well-being. But the nature of that participation has yet to be fully explored. To be sustainable, this participation must be substantive and creative; it must allow the people themselves to have access to knowledge and the use of appropriate technology. Currently, in some parts of the world, the restricted participation of women is a severe barrier to the decision-making process and hence increasing the production level. When women's capacity is used effectively physically, intellectually and morally, they can participate fully in the community's social life. Sustainability requires women and men to have equal opportunities in all social and economic development activities. Therefore, the grass root population must be at the centre of developmental activities.

The Market

Products produced by business organisations then move to different types of needs and wants to be distributed. A market is where buyers and sellers exchange goods and services. Thus, an effective relationship between buyers and sellers is essential for market management and achieving performance. The benefits are numerous if the markets are organised, controlled, developed and regulated correctly. It leads to more interactions and cooperation among people and nations. In particular, developing countries will have a more significant opportunity to sell their products locally, nationally, regionally and globally. The process reduces the gap between those experiencing poverty and those experiencing affluence leading to economic and environmental sustainability.

However, several factors are necessary for an effective and fair trade among nations. One is the equilibrium of interests. The market will be balanced when consumers and producers are satisfied, the environment is protected, and future generations are respected. Also, wage systems can damage the market if they are above or below the market equilibrium wage. Although some of these issues are meant for the distant future, the more immediate plan should be to increase the knowledge and information of individuals or groups that directly or indirectly influence the size and effectiveness of the market. For example, all professions in the market – including journalism, advertising, insurance, banks, financers and investors must have a transparent, professional and ethical code of conduct that its members must observe. It is now the time that the system of a free-market economy becomes controlled, regulated and even restricted. It is now a window of opportunity for the governments, the banking system, and the insurance industry to fix the economy by re-establishing a 'code of honour'.

An essential aspect of the modern market is the globalisation and harmonisation of market activities. The main economic implication of globalisation is that economic activities in different markets become coordinated.

Distribution

How do we get from our present condition to more sensible, equitable, sustainable, and prosperous communities? The response to this question requires an effective allocation of resources rather than the normal distribution currently used. This means a universal standard of justice and fairness should be incorporated in all phases of the cycle of production. Though efficiency is essential, it is not the only economic goal of the market. Economic efficiency and fairness should go hand in hand. Thus, our challenge of sustainability is more in productivity and market efficiency than it is in the effective distribution of income and wealth to enable all citizens to have the ability to obtain goods and services.

Another aspect of distributive justice is regarding the social function of wealth. Ideally, the profit earned must be reinvested for development and job creation and not accumulated in the hands of a few. For example, spending on education and training is an excellent sensible cost. However, spending on armaments is a dire bad cost. The guiding principles affecting distributive justice suitable for sustainability are the rearrangement of human livelihood and the social economy.

Consumption

Consumption destroys the act of production, and the cycle of production repeats itself. Consumer society or consumerism is the greatest challenge of our time. We should make a distinction between consumerism and living well. The perspective is living well with moderation. Society should be prosperous, while individuals should be content with little/moderation. Of course, content with a minor may have implications in line with sustainable economic activity. Viewed only from a financial perspective, it means less consumption, which may affect employment, income, investment, and other aspects crucial to economic development and well-being. Reducing consumption by developed nations means less export by developing countries and thus affecting their already fragile economic well-being. However, it can also be argued that content with a minor and distributing the extra available resources to lower income groups. Sustainability does not reduce economic activity but makes it more maintainable and justifiable. This happens because the increase in the economy caused by the lower income group is more than the decrease caused by reducing consumption by the higher income group. This is true because most of the world's population lives in developing countries and is considered lower-income. In this way, the living standards of the generality of the people improve and lead to universal prosperity, an essential element of sustainability.

The assumption is that in an ideal market situation, those damaging and unnecessary goods and services that are not in line with human dignity and are harmful to the ecosystem will be eliminated. Some, however, may wonder what the replacement for the economic losses of such elimination will be. The perspective here is that for advancing civilisation and considering the nobility of human beings, there will be opportunities for creating alternative job prospects for producing goods and services befitting human nobility.

Achieving a balanced eco-system

On the one hand, the goal of economic growth is considered one of the important indicators to check a country's development level. On the other hand, the eco-system issue has become increasingly heated in today's world, where all countries are looking for economic growth and development and trying to progress daily. There have been many questions regarding the effects of economic development on the environment in recent times. With the increase of greenhouse gases such as methane, carbon dioxide, water vapour and nitrogen oxide in the earth's atmosphere, the earth's temperature has increased, which has caused unpleasant changes in the environment. Economic growth and increased production require more use of natural resources and energy, especially fossil fuels, which in turn leads to the destruction of the environment. Since one of the features of our world is competition, the expansion of business development without an environmental approach will seriously endanger people's lives worldwide and cause an imbalance in using the earth's precious resources. Therefore, to solve environmental crises, societies should consider the development of environmental protection programs and the development process in line with the attention to the safety of the ecosystem. Businesses should benefit from the emergence of more advanced knowledge and technologies to achieve sustainability when planning business objectives.

Moreover, economic development is not a unilateral force. Economic development affects a wide range of economic and non-economic behaviours in different ways. Despite this, it leaves a different impact on the quality of the environment. For example, economic growth based on production usually leads to an increase in air pollution, but the large expansion of the service sector may have little impact on air pollution. It should be remembered that economic development is a multi-dimensional and broad concept that automatically opens and advances wide-ranging economic aspects for society. Economic development increases household income and improves physical infrastructure. Each development structure can increase or decrease the rate of environmental degradation. Accordingly, even considering the economic development unit by unit and their relationship with the environmental situation is a delicate relationship.

A large amount of research conducted in this field has moved towards using development components and their impact on the environment to establish a connection between economic development and the environment. These researches have focused on the issue of which components of economic development have a favourable impact on the environment and which components have an adverse impact on the environment. In this context, it is possible to name five main cases as the most important possible economic factors, which are:

- changes in consumption due to increased income
- better access to capital

- advancement of technology and infrastructure
- Commercial freedom and market competition
- Reducing population growth in many countries.

Conclusion

Creating a sustainable lifestyle after COVID-19 requires a more sensible and equitable condition. The application of various elements of sustainability smooths the economic transition to a better future for all. Social, economic, and political activities must work appropriately in three parts: first, preserving resources. This means protecting and improving the resources needed to create prosperity, including human, physical and natural resources. Second, processing production. This means converting resources into usable products, including goods and services; only valuable products can be considered economic goods and services. Third, fair distribution of resources, which means distributing goods and services fairly and justly among all citizens.

Chapter 3 -
Globalisation requires a solid foundation

Introduction

Even though the definition of globalisation has been attempted by many authors and researchers on the topic, the word continues to mean different things to different people. Considering this, I do not try any general definition of globalisation. Rather, I explain the term in the context of sensible, equitable and sustainable principles leading us to a transition with a prosperous global economy. I will view globalisation beyond limited economic aspects of life that considers it a 'borderless market' or 'free movement of resources across nations' or 'closer integration of countries and peoples of the world culturally and politically.'

Divers interpretations

Every age has its challenges. Two hundred fifty years ago, the challenge was to promote and humanise the first industrial revolution for Western Europe and the USA. One hundred fifty years ago, the main challenge was to create a safe and liveable urban environment as industrial cities began to expand.

Ninety years ago, the main challenge was to overcome the great depression of the 1930s. Fifty years ago, the challenge was making the world more sustainable. Today our main challenge is creating a purposeful globalisation based on the standard of justice.

Globalisation expert Shapoor Rassekh[4] considers the increasing interconnectedness of humanity a 20th-century phenomenon. Suppose we define globalisation as the interdependency of all nations, as a borderless society for businesses, and as coming together as citizens of one globe. In that case, globalisation is a modern idea. In other words, the way we understand and define the world as one globe is a 20th-century experience, and there are several reasons for this claim:

- The North and South Poles were founded in the late 19th and early 20th centuries. Therefore, the entire globe is complete and is known to us in the 20th century.

- An essential aspect of globalisation is communication among people around the globe. Effective communication among people and nations started in the 20th century with the invention of information technology. Technological changes connect people and countries, including the internet, mobile telephones, and digital electronics.

- Also, an essential part of globalisation is the openness of people and nations to accept it. Globalisation is of interest to this generation, especially the younger ones. Leaders with more optimistic views, such as promoting unity and cooperation, and supporting human rights, have become more popular. At the same time, those not practising these principles have become isolated.

- The rise of Asia within the global economy, including India, China, and the tiger economies. A Tiger economy is another name for Southeast Asia's newly developed and industrialised economies, including Singapore, Hong Kong, Taiwan, and South Korea.

- It is becoming increasingly clear that the world has reduced to a global village; in an ideal sense, the village represents humanity. These changes have made our world smaller, and hence it was easy; for example, for coronavirus to spread fast throughout the world without consideration of any border limitations. With this Pandemic, some challenges and problems of contemporary globalisation are understood, and the new awareness about sensible and sustainable globalisation based on interdependency, collaboration, consideration and sympathy is shaping.

This type of globalisation, however, has created a paradox. The paradox is that, on the one hand, due to advanced information and technology, increased capital, and better and cheaper transport systems, food production has increased substantially; on the other hand, one billion people go hungry every night.

The current type of globalisation, however, has created a paradox. The paradox is that, on the one hand, due to advanced information and technology, increased capital, and better and cheaper transport systems, food production has increased substantially; on the other hand, millions of people go hungry every night.

Looking at the transition of the history of economic thoughts, a different perspective of new globalisation is possible. In the last two-three hundred years, it has been noted that economic ideas are always and intimately a product of their own time and place. For example, the views of Adam Smith[5] are in the context of the early trauma of the Industrial Revolution, those of Karl Marx[6] were in the era of uncontrolled capitalist power, and those of John Maynard Keynes[7] were a response to the disaster of the Great Depression (1927-1933). Looking from this perspective, globalisation is a distinguishing characteristic of our time.

Global imbalances

An essential aspect of the modern market is the globalisation of market activities. Goods and services once produced in industrialised countries are now made much cheaper and more efficient elsewhere. This is now possible because trade liberalisation, global financial interdependency, reduced transport costs and information technology have enabled the free movement of labour and capital in different parts of the globe. However, shaping the future global economy needs to be revised. In principle, the new globalisation has caused global imbalances. Examples of global imbalances include global current account imbalances due to trade imbalances, imbalances in consumption and production of CO_2, or the situation where some countries have more wealth than others leading to widening the gap between the rich and the poor. The recent International Monetary Fund's External Sector Report highlighted the persistence of imbalances and a switch of imbalances towards advanced economies.[8] These are just a few examples of global imbalances.

Of course, the transition towards a future global economy is complex; it passes through stages, and we sometimes experience unpleasant situations. Thus, imbalances are an ongoing part of the process. We need to reprocess global social, political and financial arrangements with effective moral leadership on the part of all participants. There are several causes for imbalances in the market and the economy, including lack of effective leadership, lack of cooperation, political disunity, self-interest, and no global vision. Thus, we see that economics is only one aspect of imbalances. At the international level, there is a need for coordination of political unity. Several imbalances are barriers to an ideal global economy for the future. The followings are a few recommendations for a more balanced economy:

• There is a need for a balance of benefits or a more effective distribution of the earth's resources among peoples of the world. The emphasis should be on balancing benefits with a productive contribution to society, considering humanitarian standards and values.

• There is a need for a balance of decision-making. All nations must have representatives to discuss issues that affect their lives. The grass root population must have a voice in decision-making.

- The need for a balance of trade relations. This leads to more interactions and cooperation among people and nations. The least developed countries should have more opportunities to sell their product globally.

- There is a need for a balance between the agricultural and manufacturing sectors of the economy. These two sectors are interdependent. The least developed economies must have advanced know-how and appropriate technology to expand the agriculture and manufacturing sectors. Creating a balance of proper technology and know-how globally is essential for economic development in developing countries.

- To acquire the necessary skills, there is a need to balance education and training. Universal education and training in all countries will increase productivity and facilitate labour movement from countries with a surplus of skilled labour to countries with shortages.

- There is a need for a balanced usage of the world's natural resources. This will enable countries with an absence or shortage of resources to increase their output.

- There is a need for a balance of international financial regulation so that countries with a shortage of funds will have access to funds necessary for development.

- To be a part of the global market, developing countries should be able to produce products suitable for local and international markets. For this to happen, a regulated global market is necessary.

- Human nature is both material and spiritual; thus, there is a need to balance these two aspects of life. The aim of economics and spirituality is the same: advancing people's quality of life. To achieve this, the material and spiritual parts of our lives must go hand in hand.

Challenges

Debates on globalisation, especially in policy-making circles, are often shaped by national interests, whether social, economic, or political. However, if the fundamentals of globalisation were to be carefully examined, it would be broader than policies that are of specific interest to one nation but would appropriately be extended to consider all aspects of our global life in a changing world.

The challenge to early humanity was the family's survival; today's challenge is how to shape the future global economy or tie together the new globalisation.

Massive changes in communication and information technology, low-cost and advanced transportation and global financial interdependency have guaranteed that the future of economic life is global. This is the direction of our life, and it seems there are no other alternatives to it. However, negotiating the path to the future depends on several forces, including governments, industrialised countries, multinational corporations and individuals, pressure groups and non-governmental organisations. Each of these forces brings an economic perspective to the global negotiating network and shapes the future of global society. Does this formula of shaping globalisation create a kind of economy that accords with the standards of justice? One thing that needs to be more clearly addressed by experts in shaping our future is the significance of human values in providing an underlying motivation and direction to create a just global economy. The current shape of globalisation will produce a few significant challenges, including:

The challenge of environmental degradation or excessive pressure on the physical planet: The fact that the current globalisation of affairs affecting the environment cannot be denied. Two leading causes of environmental degradation and global warming must be dealt with. One is consumerism, and the other is the economic growth of industrialised nations and emerging economies or newly developed countries affecting the environment globally. Any reform or alternative to replacing the present systems must be long-term, global, sustainable, sensible, responsive, equitable, with balanced growth, and considering human values. The challenge is how we can get to such a desired position. Ethical transformation is therefore required before we can expect any substantial progress.

Challenges of inequality: Critics of current globalisation consider inequality as its essential component and its impact on poverty. Globalisation has increased the gap between the rich and poor between and within both developed and developing countries. Joseph Stiglitz believes this type of globalisation has created rich countries with poor people. Such challenges are centred mainly on economic justice. Economic justice in different research fields may have different meanings and understandings. Here it has been referred to as the disparity between the rich and the poor. Economic justice is, therefore, removing the financial gap between different strata of society.

According to Amartya Sen, economic inequality has different parts. In one part, we can discuss income inequality; in another, we can discuss wealth inequality. But the main issue is inequality's impact on the health of people in a society. The increase in class differences and the huge difference in the level of people's access to economic services is what causes people's mental health to be affected. We are witnessing people who are with an increasing effort to enjoy the minimum standards of life compared to those who have maximum services due to their large wealth. In this situation, the motivation to work and effort is lost, and social crimes increase. In such a society, the process of economic development is done slowly. On the other hand, this difference in financial power also causes a difference in the availability of educational, medical and health services, all of which cause tension and anxiety in society and gradually destroy the unity of the nation. Inequality has very wide dimensions and does not include only economic and financial issues. Sometimes this is gender equality, and sometimes equality includes the existence of necessary services for all sections of society.

Other challenges corresponding to globalisation include consumerism, demographic change, unfair international trade, aggressive competition, financial crises, poor governance, violence, human displacement, and domestic social and political problems. Also, it is essential to note that sometimes, the means of uniting humanity can act as a dis-unifying force. For example, information technology may also promote a faster spread of hate and fear.

Globalisation has created both economic opportunities and challenges, including:

- On the one hand, the flow of goods and services provides consumers with more choices and lower prices. On the other hand, consumerism has caused a waste of resources and has had widespread environmental consequences for the earth.
- Labour migration can lead to the transfer of human resources from low-productivity areas to efficient production areas and cause better resource allocation, leading to increased production. But at the same time, the migration and movement of populations have economic, social and political other consequences.
- On the one hand, increasing the incorporation of financial markets at the international level has caused the transfer of resources towards efficient production. This has improved the economy of some nations. But on the other hand, it has made national policy-making incapable of targeting macroeconomic

variables such as inflation and made economies more vulnerable to global financial crises.

- The increase in the integration of global markets and the distribution of the production process of goods has increased productive efficiency, providing opportunities to earn more in developing countries. As a result, reducing poverty in some parts of the world. However, the supply chain structure of goods against crises such as COVID-19 has become vulnerable in developing countries.

As a result, developing countries with appropriate policies can benefit from opportunities provided by globalisation. The developing nations should open their borders to global trade, both at the level of trade in goods and services and at the level of greater financial integration. The policies must lead to economic growth, increase welfare, and reduce poverty and inequality.

Various reactions

Supporters of globalisation argue that it is beneficial to all people and nations. The argument is that there is nothing wrong with the idea of globalisation. What is wrong is that its benefits have yet to be distributed among all fairly and justly. It also can be argued that globalisation has made the world too competitive, and in a heavily competitive market, weaker nations with no competitive capability would suffer. It becomes even more severe if developing countries don't have access to sufficient resources to achieve decent economic development. These include skilled labour, natural resources, advanced technology, and enough capital to be invested. Also, having access to information technology enables them to gather the required information about global prices. The future global economy must consider these factors to sustain fairness for developing countries. Once they have greater access to a worldwide market to sell their products, their governments will receive more revenue for improving public services. Since globalisation increases economic growth, and an increase in economic growth reduces poverty, there is a connection between globalisation and poverty reduction.

The current transition for shaping the global economy could be more sensible, equitable and pleasing to the developing world. Let us, for example, look at the kinds of trade between wealthy industrialised nations and developing countries. The exchange between a rich and a developing country may prevent developing countries from expanding their industrial base because rich countries export manufactured items while developing countries export agricultural output. As long as this trade relationship persists, the developing countries will produce only agricultural goods. Since labour productivity increases faster in manufacturing than agriculture, this trade benefits the wealthy and manufacturing countries more than the developing countries, leading to greater income inequality. The nations known as 'the Tiger Economies' or the 'New Developed Economies' realised this and moved their economies from agriculture to more manufacturing sector. Tiger Economy describes several growing economies in Southeast Asia, including Singapore, Hong Kong, South Korea, and Taiwan.

Solid foundations

In any discussion of globalisation, the elements of being sensible, equitable, sustainable and purposeful should be considered. A materialistic approach to globalisation ignores the true reality of human nature and thus fails to attract the motivational powers of the human spirit, which begins with a moral framework. Understanding the issue from this perspective helps to overcome the challenges of achieving an ideal globalisation.

Unity is the missing part of the formula for the transition to sensible and sustainable globalisation. This principle is the distinguishing characteristic of an approach to purposeful globalisation. Unity in an economic sense is an agreement in a way that people are concerned, interconnected and responsible for the needs of each other, recognise human well-being as a human right and accept that the suffering of others will affect their comfort in the long run. Thinking of humanity as one entity, whether in a small community or the wider society, can be effective in resource efficiency.

A significant subject pertinent to globalisation is the interdependence of people and nations. Nations increasingly realise that interdependency is a prerequisite for their future prosperity and consequently realise that self-sufficiency is no longer possible. In light of this discussion, the following definition by an expert in globalisation, Sohail Boshruei, conveys an appropriate description of globalisation:

> Globalisation is a vision of world unity in so deep and broad a sense as to embrace every aspect of human life. However, such a vision of planetary unity and integration bears no relation to the often bland, faceless, and amoral global marketplace we see operating today. Instead, it recognises and

celebrates the rich diversity of creeds and cultures while affirming humankind's unity. The approach to globalisation can be summed up as a commitment to the concept of unity in diversity and what this practice entails in the life of the individual and society alike.[9]

On a more encouraging and promising condition, humanity has realised the need to unite people and nations. In other words, the concept of unity has been recognised in theory. Annually, many international conferences are organised by the United Nations and governments to discuss issues related to humanity because we have understood that living in isolation is impossible. Any transition to a better future must consider that we are interconnected in every aspect: socially, economically, environmentally, and morally. It is realised that we live in an age where the oneness of humanity is not an option; it is a necessary condition for survival. Humanity struggles to form an ideal and meaningful society based on love and unity.

With unity, the benefits of globalisation will be distributed more fairly among world citizens. Unity and eliminating all prejudices lead to mutual trade, economic growth, and job creation. Therefore. with unity, resources will be allocated more efficiently, resulting in maintaining global economic sustainability, which is protecting the Earth's resources for improving the life of this generation and future generations.

Unity versus Oneness

Although unity and oneness are used interchangeably in many cases, they differ. Some of the differences are shown below:

- Unity is the catalyst or a bridge to strengthen oneness, and it can be achieved through various processes, for example, decision-making through a democratic and consultative method. Oneness, on the other hand, is the outcome of the unity of thoughts through consultative decision-making. Also, in unity, people gather for a common interest, such as discussing environmental issues, concerns related to the refugee crisis, or eradicating poverty. These events and activities are processes of integration that, if done sincerely and adequately, leads to unity of thoughts and strengthen the oneness of humanity.

- Unity is a temporary connection based on a common interest in a group. Oneness is an actual integration of the whole. In other words, the term unity suggests the idea of a group of individuals coming together for a common goal. A group may think alike but differ in personality and views. Oneness is created by integrating the group with a spirit of love, fellowship, and unity. At that moment, there is no identity other than the condition that they are all ONE in spirit.

- Unity should be the vision at the start of any activity, to finish it with oneness. This is a big challenge as many activities with good intentions fail. The absence of precise planning, and lack of resources, including human, physical and financial, are some of the challenges that may exist in strengthening oneness.

- Unity is the means that lead to the transformation of human relationship and ends with oneness. All events and activities should have a sufficient follow-up that allows oneness to develop. For an effective relationship between all participants in a community, morality becomes a fundamental principle for its operation.

Of course, the core principle of unity can be challenged because, currently, there are many obstacles to the transformation of consciousness, such as doubts, misconceptions, prejudices, suspicions, and narrow self-interest. Such challenges require society to change its attitudes before finding solutions for creating sensible globalisation. Although there are challenges, we should be in a dynamic state of transformation with a culture of learning and confidence facing challenges. This approach promotes the positive change of individuals and families into a new generation. One such method is understanding human nature, which encourages us to re-examine ourselves and our purpose in life. Today the effects of the gradual application of the spirit of unity, such as the rejection of racial prejudices, the greater awareness of the need to protect the environment, the recognition of a need for political unity, migration and the refugee crisis have led to recognise positive aspects of human potential, recognising principles of spirituality to reduce absolute poverty, the acceptance of gender equality in many societies, and the greater awareness of human rights, are apparent on the broader community. The recognition and application of these measures would gradually strengthen the principle of oneness.

Conclusion

It should be noted that economics is a means to the main goal, which is the creation of sensible, equitable and sustainable globalisation. However, such a vision of purposeful globalisation has little to do with today's often insensitive, unethical, corrupt economics. One of the applications of the principle of ideal globalisation is to coordinate human, financial and physical resources for the general benefit of market participants in a fair and just way. Therefore, the term 'justice' can be referred to as a method of achieving social-political-economic objectives.

In this discussion, a new concept of the economy is stated as one of the important principles of ideal globalisation, and the function of economics is not necessarily about prices, supply, demand, goods and services. These, and many more economic variables, are just the means to understand the end. Economics is about the relationship between people, and it is about people's behaviour. It is the relationship between buyers and sellers, between a government and citizens, between bankers and those who apply for bank loans, between employees and employers, and it is about owners of small firms and those of multinational organisations. And when we talk about the relationship and behavioural components between human beings, ethical principles play an important role.

Chapter 4 - Ending poverty

Introduction

Poverty is one of the biggest challenges our world faces today and, if not ended, will put globalisation in an extremely difficult position. There are many reasons that eradicating poverty is for the benefit of the whole society. Accepting that poverty exists when we know it is not morally right is wrong. Poverty reduction is good for democracy. People who are poor cannot participate in political decision-making. Ending poverty can lead to the reduction of violence and conflict among people and even among countries. Reducing poverty causes more participation of the poor in economic life, which increases activities in the whole market, including production, distribution and consumption. For these and many other related reasons ending poverty is one of the issues that are at the top of the agenda of governments and most international organizations.

Concepts and definitions

In the economic textbooks, the word poverty has been defined. However, in real life, poverty cannot be defined. One should experience it to see how devastating life is. It is often puzzling to economists to hear people refer to globalisation as 'worsening poverty' even when the total number of people in poverty has fallen significantly. Part of the explanation for this puzzling view is that many people consider the phrase 'worsening poverty' to be apposite in any situation where many already poor people are made poorer. Thus, it may be applied even when the number of impoverished people has decreased.

Many people think that poverty is like what we see in some movies or TV series, a small house, a working father, a mother with low expectations, a simple life without luxury and happy and contented children. But poverty means debt and late instalments. It means enduring a toothache, working the whole day. It means more of your salary goes for rent, loans, and medicine. It means that you are in the heat of summer and the cold of winter. Go on foot or by bus and stay on the road for hours. Poverty means the stress of your belongings. It means not being able to take a simple meal, it means your fridge only has bread and cheese, it means your child's shoes are torn, but you can't do anything, It means being depressed and angry, but you don't have money for counselling, it means to endure every insult and humiliation in the work environment because you need a few secrets of your rights, it means to fall in love, but you don't have money for a date, or you say let me not make someone else miserable.

Millions of people have come out of poverty in the last few decades. China is anticipating having zero absolute poverty by 2030. Though this is great news, such a poverty reduction is limited to a few countries, including India and China. This is significant because poverty has not been reduced evenly in all countries. According to Joseph Stiglitz, Africa is forgotten and must be remembered in any future globalisation.

The issue of poverty is a complex issue that should be looked at from several angles, including economic, historical, social, psychological, and spiritual deprivation. Regarding historical poverty, some people believe that poverty has always existed and that it is not a new thing and is considered normal. They argue that poverty is like war, and we have always had war; war is normal, and peace is abnormal. Of course, most people do not agree with this way of thinking. We live in an age where we can produce voluminous goods and services with new knowledge and technology. In such a situation where mass production occurs, and consumerism is one of the challenges of our time, talking about poverty and hunger should not have a place in society. Therefore, poverty should be considered abnormal and eliminated globally.

The global solution to each problem, including poverty, depends on other issues. Solving one problem, ignoring others, and leaving them alone is impossible. We know that when the United Nations was formed, it aimed to work for world peace and maintain it. But they realised it was impossible to establish peace and leave other problems alone. Therefore, they could not achieve their goal.

Consequently, they gradually expanded the scope of their goals, and now they are involved in other activities such as environment, human rights, and economic and social development. The poverty crisis is also included in the guidelines of the United Nations. Therefore, we see that the reason for not eradicating absolute poverty is that we want to do it only from an economic perspective.

In contrast, poverty has a multi-dimensional root. It should be addressed from a historical, cultural, social, economic, and environmental point of view and an ethical perspective. More than general solutions are needed to fight poverty individually. The problem of poverty is different in every country. For example, the nature of poverty is different in the USA, India, and

Bangladesh. In the USA, we mostly face materialism and consumerism and the feeling of not being satisfied, while in Bangladesh, we face the problem of hunger and malnutrition. In Iran, people face the problem of minimum subsistence. Therefore, a different solution should be considered for each one. A general resolution currently adopted is mainly transferring money from rich to developing countries. Unfortunately, it was seen that this program, which has been running since the time the UN was established, has not only not eliminated poverty but has also made some developing countries dependent on rich countries.

To compare income and wealth, two points should be considered. First, because wealth accumulates over time, it is placed on average at a higher income level. Second, the inequality of wealth distribution is greater than the inequality of income distribution. This issue is vital because wealth alone can generate income; therefore, as wealth inequality increases, income inequality also increases. Since wealth is the source of investment, rising inequalities mean a widening gap between rich and poor people in their ability to take advantage of investment opportunities.

On the other hand, measuring income (and wealth) inequality is difficult. The most used index in the literature is the Gini coefficient, but it should be noted that this coefficient gives only a part of the overall picture. Specifically, the Gini coefficient is a general measure of how income is distributed, but it doesn't show, for example, what percentage of people can't afford their basic needs. For this purpose, inequality indicators are usually reported together with poverty indicators.

The responsibility of a government

Individual governments in both developed and developing countries must adopt policies for reducing poverty. These include:

- Creating work and employment
- Creating suitable jobs with high income
- Increasing social welfare and access to social benefits
- Investing in high-quality education for children
- Laws against any discrimination
- Redistribution of wealth from people with high incomes to people with lower incomes (fair tax system).
- Increasing economic inclusion
- Creating equal opportunities for all citizens

- Planning monetary and financial policies for the benefit of the poor
- Granting microcredit finance targeting the poor

Economic growth policies for the benefit of the poor include:

- Land reforms
- Using production techniques that focus on the use of labour
- Rural and agricultural development
- Investment in rural infrastructure

A survey of religion on wealth and poverty

Religiosity is a growing phenomenon, especially among poorer societies. Jacob Olupona, an expert in African spirituality, confirms that the most impoverished people tend to be deeply spiritual in Africa.[10] Also, research carried out by two political scientists, Pippa Norris and Ronald Inglehart (2011), indicates how religion is growing, especially among poor and oppressed communities. For example, insecurity, a lack of food and survival create the seedbed for religion. Therefore, a sense of dependence among the oppressed and the poor increases religious activities. These experts found new evidence about the close correlation between poverty and religiosity in eighty societies, covering most of the world's major faiths. Based on their research, they argue that religiosity persists most strongly among vulnerable populations, especially those in poorer nations and in failed states, facing personal survival-threatening risks. They show that exposure to physical, societal and personal risks drives religiosity. Conversely, a systematic erosion of traditional religious practices, values and beliefs may have occurred among the more prosperous strata in the rich nations. But at the same time, a growing proportion of the population — in both rich and poor countries — spends time thinking about the meaning and purpose of life. It is argued that established churches are losing their ability to tell people how to live their lives in developed countries, but spiritual concerns, broadly defined, may be becoming increasingly important.[11]

Of course, it is not fair to say that religion is one of the main causes of poverty. Poverty consists of material, social, cultural, as well as spiritual. The causes of poverty can be divided into man-made and natural disaster factors, including shortage of resources, physical and human resources; political instability and internal conflict; national debt crisis; human rights issues including discrimination and social inequality; poor health-care system; unemployment; the existence of a weak and unrecognized currency in the international market; all types of natural disasters such as earthquakes and seasonal hurricanes; and social exclusion. Also, unfortunately, the poor have no opportunity for adequate education and skills learning or access to necessary resources for improvement.

Furthermore, the presence of certain values in the current economic and market condition that maintain poverty, for instance, through effective advertisement, the need is created to consume; excessive availability of credit makes it easier to buy and fall into debt; social status is constructed in terms of what one possesses. The more one possesses, the higher their social standing; the consumption-driven economy urges cheap production to participate in a competitive market. The result is the exploitation of labour and resources. These values stimulate consumption and create the illusion that increased consumption can only alleviate poverty. The more one has, the richer she/he appears, while one becomes poorer in trying to possess more. The illusion is created that a proper life is a life of consuming more goods.

Therefore, either economic condition or religion can no longer be regarded as the sole measure of poverty. Poverty entails social, cultural, economic, political, psychological, physiological and ecological factors.

Wealth and poverty

As the concept of poverty is difficult to define, the notion of wealth is also difficult to define or measure because it is mainly a stock of assets such as houses, land or personal possessions and accumulated money; therefore, it is different from income. Income is a flow, while wealth is a stock. If we define wealth as the abundance of valuable possessions and assets, then it is difficult to measure because they can be appreciated or depreciated. The question that needs to be raised is how income and wealth affect well-being, the standard of living, or creating a happy life. Gross Domestic Product (GDP) measures a country's standard of living and economic growth. However, this measurement is based solely on the monetary values of goods and services and ignores, for example, negative externalities such as the production of those unnecessary and damaging products affecting the life of humans, animals, and the environment. A 'happy life' should not be measured in terms of income alone but in terms of well-being, income being one of the features. With 'well-being', the all-encompassing levels of deprivation need to be addressed. Those values applied in current economic systems need to be revised. Values that can redirect attention away from selfishness, greed and the need to own and consume. Values such as contentment, moderation, cooperation, compassion and fairness should become part of an economic system.

The problem of wealth accumulation and its concentration in the hands of a few is expanding and keeps growing locally, nationally, and globally. As the economy grows, the concentration of private wealth gets worse. Exploring this view, Oxfam has been giving us depressing updates on wealth concentration each year. For example, they have reported that in 2010, 388 richest people in the world owned more wealth than the bottom half of the world population owned. In 2014, 85 richest people were in the same position. In 2015 the number was reduced to 80 people. In 2016, Oxfam reported that 62 richest people own more wealth than that owned by the bottom half of the world population. Therefore, the private wealth concentration is getting worse and worse each year.

This kind of wealth accumulation and its concentration in the hands of few is dangerous because it causes an imbalance in economic activities, including shortages and surpluses of products and hence wastage of resources. The concentration of wealth also means the concentration of social and political power and the concentration of privileges and opportunities. This may cause destroying harmony and democracy and pushes the world towards a social explosion. The reverse is also true, if we do not have any wealth, we have no power and privileges. According to Oxfam, the bottom 50% of the world population, owning only a small fraction of 1% of the global wealth, belong to this category. This condition cannot be continued and need to be fixed.

The concentration of wealth is an ongoing, non-stop process under the present economic system. A current economic assumption is that human happiness can be achieved merely by increasing the wealth of the individual members of society. The underlying assumption is that all human beings are motivated by selfishness and greed and that the more any particular economic policy caters for these base motivations, the more successful it will be. The self is primarily seen as someone who seeks to maximise his or her own utility, often through maximisation of consumption opportunity. The root idea flowing from self-interest is consumer sovereignty and utility maximisation. The rationale is that consumers know their interests best and can act to advance them through an exchange. For many, prosperity lies in increasing consumption, and each consumer will pursue his or her opportunities until the marginal cost of a transaction exceeds the benefits of it. Each person maximizes utility or happiness subject to a number of constraints, including income. Thus, the economic theory considers mainly monetary aspects of life and ignores other factors, such as values essential for creating relationships among people and those protecting the environment.

Let us draw our attention to the point that the richest people are not necessarily bad people, as popularly imagined; the system does it for them. Since 1776 with the publication of *The Wealth of Nations* by Adam Smith, the modern economic system or the free-market economy has been in operation, those in power and perhaps with good intentions have tried to bring a better life for the generality of the population, but the manipulation, mismanagement and abuse of systems have created a condition of widening the gap between the rich and the poor. It also can be argued that wealthy people have enormous political power and influence and do not allow decision-makers to prevent them from becoming even wealthier. The current free market system is out of control and does not convey the original message advocated by its founder, Adam Smith, in his book, *The Theory of Moral Sentiments*. In this book, Smith discusses the position of philosophers and those in charge of society. He argues that it would be contradictory and unjust for them to think about their own self-interest. Instead, they should cultivate a sense of public duty to be good at helping solve the world's most pressing problems. This vital and critical idea of the founder of the free-market system is forgotten. There is a need for a new way of thinking to change the economic structure of the whole society. The current market system needs to be controlled, coordinated, and even regulated, and absolute freedom in an economic system leads to confusion and corruption.

Concerning the issue of poverty, the current process of globalisation, although defective in many ways, is one reason for poverty reduction. The UN expects to end poverty by 2030. This is an excellent news. The worry is that poverty reduction has not occurred evenly across the globe. For example, as Joseph Stiglitz noted:

> The current process of globalisation is generating unbalanced outcomes, both between and within countries. Wealth is being created, but too many countries and people are not sharing in its benefits. They also have little or no voice in shaping the process. Seen through the eyes of the vast majority of women and men, globalisation has not met their simple and legitimate aspirations for decent jobs and a better future for their children. Many of them live

in the limbo of the informal economy without formal rights and in a swathe of poor countries that subsist precariously on the margins of the global economy. Even in economically successful countries, some workers and communities have been adversely affected by globalisation. Meanwhile, the revolution in global communications heightens awareness of these disparities... these global imbalances are morally unacceptable and politically unsustainable.[12]

Another worrying fact is that increasing the wealth of the rich is much steeper than the decline of the poverty level. This has caused an increasing gap between the rich and the poor.

Conclusion

Balancing the fair distribution of the Earth's resources is morally and economically cherished. Unjust economic conditions can threaten peace and security; poverty is the most severe and keeps the world unstable. Mahatma Gandhi said, 'Poverty is the most serious violence, and Muhammad Yunus said, 'Poverty is a threat to peace.' Gandhi and Yunus are from the grass root population and understand the link between poverty and violence very well. Yunus believes that poverty is the absence of certain human rights. The frustration, hostility, hunger and anger generated by abject poverty cannot sustain peace in any society. To build a stable peace, we must find ways to provide opportunities for people to live decent and everyday lives. This requires balancing the fair distribution of the Earth's resources among people and nations. Currently, there are imbalances in the economy. This threatens peace and keeps the world in a state of volatility. Therefore, ending poverty is a priority for both the poor and the rich.

Chapter 5 -
Emerging values for the future global economy

Introduction

Emerging values for shaping a future global economy raises several questions. Why should we care about the future? Why should we care for others? Why should we care for the environment? The answer to these questions and many more causes disagreement, and we need help from experts to come forward and debate and offer solutions. Global economic problems are complex, and neither current economic systems nor short-run government plans have offered suitable solutions for shaping a future global economy. Today international economics is too complicated, and its problems cannot be solved with short-term government policies and one-dimensional solutions, mainly with monetary policies. However, identifying global challenges and having a long-term vision helps find the right path to the future.

Values are relative and a matter of opinion and judgement; they are a matter of right and wrong. Thus, ethical economics is unlike engineering, physics, and accounting, with specific procedures and facts to decide. Ethical economics should help policymakers to make better decisions, but this is different from making the right decision. For example, the government referred to its decision to reduce the budget deficit as a 'fair' policy.' Here, the term fair is a value judgement. Fair to whom? Or about the distribution of income and wealth, experts describe it as giving each one what they are 'due'. Again, here we see an element of value judgement; the dilemma is what is 'due'.

In addition to universal values that affect humanity, this chapter suggests some aspects of a new economic system appropriate for shaping the future global economy. In many instances, historically, external forces have been the grounds for establishing new values. For example, our values during the slavery period are different from those of the industrialisation period and the current values of globalisation.

We also need to look at the factor of sustainable transition when discussing the future global economy. The change process shapes human affairs, indicating that the transition to a global society is inevitable. A significant challenge in this transition is creating conditions for social and economic justice and equity among and within the nations of our global community so that humanity may benefit from the advantages of globalisation.

From around the 1970s, the world witnessed three global changes:

i) Technological changes, including the Internet, mobile telephone, and digital electronic age.

ii) The rise of Asia within the global economy, including India, China, 'Tiger Economies'[13] and BRIC[14] economies.

iii) Newly emerging global ecological crises. One of the most significant challenges of such changes is their environmental effect. According to Jeffrey Sachs (2012), the world may lose from globalisation if the rising income in emerging economies leads to global ecological calamity. These variations cause massive ongoing changes in lifestyle and a shift in income, jobs, and investment worldwide.

In modern times, international development has created favourable conditions for reinforcing common interests for a global family and global cooperation to create a better world for all its citizens. The capacity to think globally has increased, especially among the younger generation with a worldwide consciousness of knowledge, attitudes and skills needed for the proper functioning of meaningful integration, a prerequisite for a more sensible and equitable transition to globalisation.

The values referred to above about family members are personal values that find their expression in the behaviour of individuals. However, a society can also incorporate its values into its institutional structures, such as legislative and justice systems; forms of governance; social, economic, and educational structures. One of the problems in present Western society is that there is often a considerable gap between the values held by individuals and the values for which economic and social institutions are held accountable. This is particularly true of businesses in the private sector, for which profitability is often the only required value. Governments often legislate other obligations at the national level, but there needs to be a mechanism to impose any values on multinational corporations or international economic activity. Why, for example, do some of these giant corporations become extremely large that once they go bankrupt, the whole society would suffer? Any significant advance towards sustainability must address all market actors with values underlying the individual behaviour of producers and consumers and the institutional behaviour of both the public and private sectors.

The 2008 global financial crisis has raised the awareness of nations and policymakers that difficulties and challenges in one country could affect the rest of the world. Regardless of the uncertainty in the immediate future, nations and peoples are now realising that we are connected in all aspects of life. However, the current national or international institutions cannot address the underlying causes of the financial crisis that has created enormous pressure and stress. What national and international agencies such as the 'European Central Bank and the 'Bank of England' and 'The International Monetary Fund' have done so far is to repair the financial crises with their short-term policies, mainly by manipulating the monetary policies. They did not, however, identify the root cause of the problems, and because the problems are fixed on the surface, they may return anytime. This happened in the 1930s during the great depression when policymakers used money-oriented short-term policies to deal with the crisis. These agencies are doing a one-dimensional solution only through material means called 'quantitative easing, which is by printing more money, borrowing more, and lending more. The five structural root causes of the 2008 financial crisis were a mixture of monetary and non-monetary factors, including poor governance, mismanagement of monetary policy, imbalances in global trade management, mismanagement of world resources, and absence of moral values.

As stated earlier, globalisation is no longer a fantasy. It is happening whether we want it or not. If globalisation is a fact, it requires a commitment – it is necessary to work towards its creation more actively, sensibly and responsibly. The active participation of grass root population in decision-making is crucial, and promoting a consultative decision-making method at all levels is a key factor. In the global context, the participation of women in social, economic, and political activities becomes a moral obligation, and eliminating all kinds of prejudices is vital for removing barriers to development globally. The individual must be at the centre of the development process and decision-making. Development planning in the past century has mostly excluded ordinary people from participating in significant decisions that affect their lives. Their choices are often made for them by outside agencies in which they cannot play a part and are determined by goals that may conflict with their perceptions of reality. If individuals are a part of the problem, they must also be a part of the solution.

This is possible by being informed, taking responsibility, taking action, re-examining lifestyle, and involving others in the planning and decision-making.

Conclusion

We conclude this chapter with a comment from two experts in globalisation, Farhad Rassekh and John Speir. "Since economic globalisation affects people's economic lives, it has moral implications that often take centre stage in any discussion on globalisation ... If globalisation improves the lives of people, in particular, those of the least advantaged in developing countries, then the policy is not only morally desirable but imperative."[15]

Chapter 6 -
Justice in a world of injustices

Part One: Economic Justice
Part Two: Justice in the financial institutions

Part One: Economic Justice

Introduction

Justice and its connection with economics in transition and to the fundamental principle of unity and purposeful globalisation have become prominent among contemporary thinkers. Justice has been vital since the dawn of civilisation and continues to play a critical role in creating a better world for all. However, applying principles of justice has become the defining challenge as society becomes more interdependent and social, political and economic issues have become more complex. The societal emphasis is that justice is a set of moral principles for building institutions. At the individual level, the goal is to create opportunities for each person to generate a good foundation for a dignified, productive, and creative life. On the other hand, unity is the foundation for establishing a desired economic justice. The emphasis will be on economic justice and its relationship with the goal of unity whilst leaving aside more philosophical aspects.

Why is there a need for justice?

Have you ever been in a situation where the injustices in society attract your attention? How do these injustices arise and what is our role in reducing or eliminating them?

A simple and logical question to begin this discussion is, why is there a need for justice? A sensible answer is that there are injustices of all kinds in the world, and we observe some daily around us. For example, injustice arises from economic exploitation, the suffering of the poor, the malnourishment of children, child labour, wage discrimination, oppression of women, relentless competition, unfair international trade, corruption, human displacement, separation from families at a young age, and much more. It is manifestly unjust for governments to spend an increasing amount of the wealth of a nation on unnecessary and destructive commodities instead of eliminating the suffering of deprived families. It is also unjust to damage our planet, which future generations have the same rights as we do and take for granted. Justice is a human virtue that makes a person socially, politically, and economically conscientious and society internally harmonious.

Injustices become barriers towards purposeful globalisation. This needs to be addressed. Humans are social beings; hence, just and meaningful globalisation is about the interconnectedness of humans and the rest of society. Globalisation generates unbalanced outcomes, creating wealth, but only a few countries share its benefits. Most developing countries need more voice in shaping the process. These global imbalances are economically unproductive, politically unsustainable, socially unacceptable, and morally wrong. Other factors are essential for reforming and reshaping the current method and processes of globalisation. Many issues must be considered, including inequality and the democratic deficit in global economic institutions, which weakens democracy in developed and developing countries. For example, the benefits of globalisation have not been distributed fairly and justly among world citizens. Consequently, the problem with the current version of globalisation is that although the idea is good, the process for achieving it is not justified.

Throughout the history of economics, the distribution of income and wealth among the members of society has been a significant concern. There has not only been a desire to explain the distribution pattern but also a belief that fundamental issues of justice and fairness are of concern. Consequently, most of the theories of economic justice focus on distributive justice. Philosophers and economists have long debated the concept of economic justice. Although what constitutes justice may vary from time to time and from culture to culture or based on historical contexts; however, all forms of justice are founded based on ethical assumptions that include ideas about fairness. Issues related to extremes of wealth and poverty and the justification of principles of equity and equality have been raised and discussed by contemporary economists and at governmental levels.

Augusto Lopez Claros and Daniel Perell raised reasonable questions to overcome some of the injustices:

There are many factors – political fracturing, social distrust, military aggression – which stand between good policies and their implementation. These barriers, factors which contribute to the lack of political will, must be overcome through the creation of enabling environments. What is the most effective system to ensure that economic justice through the reduction of inter and intra-country inequality can be realized? How can those with greater wealth – whether individuals, corporations, or nations – be encouraged to see in its redistribution the well-being of all the human family? We should naturally turn to the global financial architecture to encourage the realization of such a global economic ethic.[16]

Therefore, if economics is defined as 'the best use of resources' and justice as 'giving to each one what he or she is due', then the two principles of economics and justice are both functionally and morally partners.

Justice with a spirit of fairness

Although justice and fairness often appear together or are used interchangeably, they differ. Justice is the establishment or determination of rights according to the rules of law for society. Fairness, on the other hand, is the quality or state of being fair, and fairness is marked by impartiality, honesty, and mercy and is free from self-interest and all kinds of prejudices. Therefore, justice is specifically enjoined upon rulers of states to establish law and order in a society. In contrast, fairness is an ethical principle whose application is urged to be observed by all.

Justice can be defined as the simultaneously fair treatment of individuals in a given situation with the result that everybody gets what they deserve. The crucial ethical issue with this definition is what exactly 'fairness' means and by what standards we can decide what a person might reasonably deserve. According to Beauchamp and Bowie (1997), theories of justice typically see fairness in two main ways:

Fair procedure: Fairness is determined according to whether everyone has had an equal opportunity to achieve a just reward for their efforts (Procedural justice).

Fair outcomes: Fairness is determined according to whether the consequences are distributed justly (Distributive justice).

Let us expand on this subject with some examples. Fairness is present in some people and absent or less in others. For instance, we say that such and such a person is fair or so and so is not fair. Here we use fairness with different meanings, primarily related to ethics. It is related to people's conscience.

In many cases, we look at our role models. For example, we should be fair, like this person or that person. This attribute should be developed and strengthened in people from childhood. On the other hand, justice is among the philosophical and legal debates that always concern philosophers, politicians, and legislators. In most cases, justice is used concerning the three principles of freedom, equal opportunities and means for advancement.

Justice is done at the community level, and fairness at the individual level. In justice, everyone gets what they deserve. In fairness, minimum welfare is created for all citizens. Justice speaks of human rights. Therefore, to create minimum welfare for everyone, it is required by legislators to make fair laws. Consequently, it is observed that the societies in which there is freedom and equal opportunities, along with the means for progress, are economically more advanced and creative.

As discussed in chapter two, one significant challenge of the current process of shaping globalisation is the disparity between the rich and the poor and the vast accumulation of excessive wealth in the hands of a few. Bearing in mind the meaning of fairness, to achieve an ideal globalisation, there is a need for fair-minded policymakers and legislators to set fair and impartial laws that provide equal opportunity for all citizens to progress. This enables people to discover their hidden talents and capabilities to become productive members of their communities.

In other words, humans are equal in the laws of the land; however, with different economic capabilities. This is a sensible way of thinking for allowing people to become active citizens not only for their own sake but also for contributing to the general well-being and prosperity.

Equality versus equity

Is social justice about equality or equity? Social justice aims for people to be equal to the law of the land. The argument is that more equal societies tend to be more creative. For example, countries which practice gender equality and religious freedom are more creative and economically more advanced. Equity is preferred when discussing economic justice from a purely monetary standpoint.

Irrespective of ideology, culture, and religion, people generally condemn extreme income inequality, which is not helping purposeful globalisation. Economic inequality is unacceptable for several reasons: inequality can be a sign of lack of opportunity; widening inequality also has significant implications for growth and macroeconomic stability, and it can concentrate on political and decision-making power in a few. Also, high and sustained levels of inequality may divert an individual's efforts toward securing favoured behaviour and protection, resulting in a misallocation of resources.

There are many advantages to lessening economic inequality, including promoting democracy, because consumers will be able to participate in economic life and increase the prosperity of an entire society. At the societal level reducing economic inequality eradicates absolute poverty, thus reducing violence within and between countries. Hence, ending economic inequality is one of the pressing issues facing global society.

Equal opportunity ensures that access to material resources is justly distributed. The view is that everyone's talents and abilities are different, and hence their economic contribution to society varies, but the opportunity should be there for all. Consequently, aside from equality in dignity and worth, human beings are not born the same. We are different in our abilities and should be different in our social and economic standing. The understanding, therefore, is that all citizens are equal in the sight of the law of the land. Government agencies should ensure that equal opportunity for progress is created for all.

The method of wealth distribution that states each according to one's ability and each according to one's productive contribution to society indicates that the provision of equal opportunity is necessary. Consequently, the wage differential which is considered as being fair is that which is based on an individual's level of education and training, capability, and talents. This is done through implementing laws, the redistribution of wealth, the creation of opportunity, the right to work, the right to education, and the right to good health.

In the past, there was a claim by critics that inequality and poverty were normal conditions and a part of human history. Indeed, short lives, limited education, health challenges, poor nutrition, limited possessions, limited mobility, and inequality suggest that, throughout history, many people have suffered from poverty. "However much such conditions are the outcome of history, they do not have to define the future, and even if current approaches to economic life satisfied humanity's stage of adolescence, they are certainly inadequate for its dawning age of maturity. There is no justification for continuing to perpetuate structures, rules, and systems that manifestly fail to serve the interests of all peoples."[17]

The role of government intervention in tackling the challenges of inequality and poverty has become crucial. The overriding priority is that appropriate legislation is required to protect the economically less advantaged people. Aside from government responsibility, the rich care for the poor. In the last hundred and fifty years, global wealth has increased substantially. We now have access to a high level of knowledge and information, technological advancement, global financial interdependency, and improved transportation. Thus, allowing poverty and extreme inequality to exist when we can address the problem is morally and economically wrong. Providing equality of educational and employment opportunities for all enables an adequate standard of living. A fair distribution of resources and eliminating extremes of wealth and poverty are the most critical part of distributive justice. Hence, economic justice involves the redistribution of income and wealth as an ideal method for reducing inequality and caring for people experiencing poverty.

Delivering justice

The belief that justice has its place in the higher nature of human beings indicates that it is innate in humans. However, efforts are needed to develop the necessary virtues for justice to become a reality. The belief in the higher nature of human beings also inspires individuals to act justly and with kindness. This can have significant implications in all aspects of socio-political-economic life. Economic justice also interlinks with the idea of overall economic prosperity. Creating more opportunities for all members of society to earn adequate wages contributes to sustained economic growth. When more citizens can maintain a steady income and provide for themselves and their families, they are more likely to spend their earnings on goods and services, which drives demand in various parts of the economy.

An outstanding attitude to guarantee a sustainable transition to just distribution of resources among the citizens of the world, in the long run, is moderation. Moderation in all aspects of life (discussed in Chapter 17) can be considered the most practical way to maintain economic justice. It maintains a balance in living a spiritual life in a material world. It is a solution to the societal problem of poverty and inequality. Moderation and development of our higher nature and economic activities can enhance human dignity, preserve the natural environment, respect future generations' rights, and advance humankind's well-being and prosperity. The idea is to attain economic sustainability and to achieve the most excellent satisfaction of needs and wants within the limits of moderation.

Role of a government in creating and maintaining economic justice

Economic justice refers to the distribution of resources and economic opportunities in society in a fair way in which all people have access to resources according to their needs. In this process, the role of the government is very crucial. The government can help create a just society by setting laws and regulations for creating employment opportunities and distributing resources fairly.

In a just economic society, people should benefit fairly and justly from the outcome of economic activities. Things like access to employment, education, health, housing, and other economic opportunities. It can be said that economic justice means more than equality in the distribution of resources. This concept not only refers to the equalisation of wealth of a nation but also emphasises the basic needs and rights of every person in the society. In other words, economic justice expresses a balance in which no person is deprived due to race, gender, religion or other personal characteristics.

Hence, the role of government is crucial in creating such an environment.

The government can play an important role in the fairer distribution of resources in society by determining distribution laws and policies, regulating the market, supporting weaker people, regulating tax and financial policies, and supporting small businesses. Also, creating job opportunities in less developed areas and providing vocational training to those in need allows people to increase their skills for improving their economic position.

The government can also play a direct role in the distribution of resources. For example, cash assistance programs to low-income households and coverage of essential services such as health and education enable the government to improve the living conditions of people in need and facilitate a more equitable distribution of resources. Other areas include building infrastructure, developing the industrial and agricultural sectors, and promoting entrepreneurship. Providing public services is another effective government responsibility for maintaining economic justice, including public infrastructure such as water, electricity, gas, and public transportation, as well as health, educational and cultural services. By providing these services fairly and equally, the government can help distribute resources fairly and give people in need the opportunity to have a better standard of living.

Conclusion

Today eighty per cent of the world's resources are distributed among twenty per cent of the population, indicating that the systems do not meet the standard of justice. This will weaken the transition to a just global society. However, according to development expert Farzam Arbab, humanity has reached a level of maturity that is "capable of developing an economy with a new logic that is not based on greed or false precepts of absolute equality, that allows reasonable freedom yet promotes and safeguards justice."[18] For economic justice to be effective, it requires a contract on the part of individuals, business organisations and governments based on fairness, compassion and cooperation. The market will function more sustainably based on these moral and spiritual principles. Once justice is applied in such an economy, every responsible agent in the market will realise that the fundamental principles of economic justice, namely, liberty, equal opportunity, and the provision of necessary means for development, are crucial in the transition of the efficient functioning of an economy.

Part Two: Justice in the financial institutions

The previous part established that the two principles of economics and justice are both functionally and morally partners. The financial market will be sustainable if these two basics go hand in hand. We must also define social justice for banking institutions because they interact with people. Social justice covers economic justice. Social justice is the virtue which guides us in creating those organised human interactions we call institutions. In turn, when justly organised, social institutions provide us access to what is suitable for the person, individually and in our associations with others. Social justice also imposes on us a responsibility to work with others to design and continually perfect our institutions as tools for personal and social development. Financial institutions, including banks and insurance companies, must be reformed with greater social responsibilities. The following recommendations are about the effective functioning of financial institutions:

• The disproportionately profit-driven economic activity of the banking system and insurance industry harms a country's poor and lower-income groups. These groups cannot survive under the policies of these institutions - which aim for profit maximisation. It is becoming increasingly evident that the solution to the banking crisis is restoring trust in financial institutions. Therefore, a total restructuring of the financial institutions is required with significant consideration of ethical values.

- Social justice and equitable growth must be top priorities for the government and financial institutions. In particular, the banking system must be assigned a significant role to achieve the objective of equitable distribution of wealth among citizens through financial inclusion. The banks must act as prime movers in the planned development process with economic growth and social justice objectives.

- The banking system, as mobilisers of savings and suppliers of credit, should play as a catalyst to increase output through capital formation. The improvement of the banking system through adjustment and regulation and the provision of funds for start-up businesses is significant.

- The banking system should act in the public interest and participate in various poverty alleviation programmes.

- A 'just and moderate interest rate' must be applied in financial transactions to facilitate the community's service and proper market functioning.

Such a policy creates an environment where there would be room for economic growth to boost confidence in the market and encourages investments by local and foreign investors.

- All professions, particularly journalists, advertising, insurance, banks, financiers and investors, should have a clear, professional, ethical code that its members must observe.

- The banking system should use a reward and punishment model. A particular reward is related to success and good performance. Punishment is related to failure and poor performance. If financial institutions follow the reward and punishment model, there is no need to pay excessive bonuses to chief executives for their poor performance and failure.

- The free-market economy system must be regulated, controlled, and reformed. This needs a concerted effort by the government, the banking system, and the insurance industry.

- To build a society based on trust, we must start in school, if not earlier. Children should learn that the noblest life is the one that produces the least misery and the most happiness in the world. This rule should also apply in business and professional life.

Conclusion

Therefore, the concept of justice is valueless if individuals, corporations, governments and the banking system are not applying fairness in contributing to poverty reduction and eliminating social unrest.

Among organisations that are so crucial for market development and sustainability are the financial system such as banking and insurance companies. These organisations' profit-driven economic activity disproportionately harms people experiencing poverty and the lower-income group. The banking system mobilises savings and acts as a supplier of credit. It should catalyse to increase output through capital formation. Banks should be engaged in acts of service to the community and participate in various poverty alleviation programmes and developmental activities.

Chapter 7 -
Is world peace possible?

Introduction

The desire for peace, which is humanity's quest, has always been in the hearts and minds of people. Today, millions of people work hard and sincerely to bring this eternal hope and desire of humanity into a reality.[19] But why are we far from this reality? War and internal conflicts are serious barriers towards a transition to economic prosperity. This chapter reflects on the question of whether world peace will ever be possible.

Five of the most important reasons that caused the fall of the Roman Empire are:

   i.   Disruption of the family foundation
   ii. Weakening of personal responsibilities
   iii. Increasing taxes and excessive government interference
   iv. Search for excessive pleasure
   v.   And the degradation of religion

If these five reasons caused the fall of the most powerful empire at a time when they did not have access to today's modern technology and telecommunication, and we are witnessing all these modern equipment today, then the possibility that society will collapse due to these causes is powerful.

More than at any other time in history, there is a need for the awareness of peace. Three situations distinguish the present from the past in increasing this awareness:

Firstly, an increase in the destructive capacity of humanity. We have never been so capable or so close to total self-destruction.

Secondly, astonishing progress has occurred in communication, transportation, and information technology. These developments have simultaneously increased and decreased the threat of war. On the one hand, little time is needed to begin a fight over misunderstandings or mistrust between two or more nations. On the other hand, little time is required to clarify the misunderstanding and resolve the mistrust if the will to do so is present.

Thirdly, the increased willingness of ordinary citizens in every country and from many diverse backgrounds to contribute, even sacrificially, to the efforts to establish meaningful and lasting world peace. In the words of Ervin Laszlo, a former member of the Club of Rome and editor-in-chief of World

Encyclopaedia of Peace, "Peace in the contemporary world is no longer an option but a necessity. All leaders and people of the world must realise this fact."[20]

Adding to the above factors, today, our world is interdependent and interrelated in every aspect. If the people of Ethiopia or Sudan suffer from hunger and malnutrition, the rest of the world feels uneasy. The refugee crisis is also a crisis for the entire humanity. The news of earthquakes, hurricanes, and other natural calamities disturbs everyone. Pain in one part of the body is the cause of pain in the rest of the body. We cannot have war and poverty in one part of the world and peace and prosperity in the rest. The COVID-19 Pandemic signals that we must see the world as one big family and that pain, suffering and restlessness in one part of the world also affect others. This is an indication that the global crisis requires global solutions. Hence, there are challenges facing humanity.

Is world peace possible?

The question of whether world peace will ever be possible can be answered by closely examining the socio-economic and political conditions of the world. The view here is not to formulate the process of establishing world peace but create awareness and understanding that having world peace is sensible, desirable and beneficial to all.

The terrifying experience as a consequence of the First World War and the Second World War is still with us. War is only one type of violence that is the cause of separation; other types of violence kill and separate people. The widening gap between the rich and poor has further divided developed and developing countries. Terrorism, human rights violation, hates campaigns, racism, family displacement, politics of fear, religious strife, family breakdown, discrimination, and injustices of all kinds are examples of chaos and separation among people. Witnessing all these injustices, we may conclude that we are not even close to achieving world peace; much must be done. The Club of Rome members Aurelio Peccei and Alexander King have described the condition of the world as follows:

Despite the wonderful body of knowledge and information he has accumulated and the means to apply it, a modern man appears to be muddling ahead as if he were blind or drugged, staggering from one crisis to another. It is increasingly evident that he is unsure where he is going or where he wants to go beyond the next few tentative steps.[21]

We may consider the current world confusion and calamities as a natural phase in an organic process leading to the unification of the entire human race. Humanity has passed through the evolutionary stages of infancy and childhood. It is now in the culminating period of its turbulent adolescence approaching its long-awaited coming of age.[22] In this organic process, steps towards world peace, especially since World War II, give hopeful signs and a sense of belonging to one global family, which has been shown in many ways. Leaders of nations talk about a new world order, economists and financial institutions talk about an international economic order, environmentalists speak about a global dimension, and our young generation talks about world citizenship. In recent years, many international conferences have been held. These are the signs that we are one step closer to world peace. In other words, the idea of world peace becomes stronger whenever a global activity is initiated. The increasing interest shown by a group of nations to formalise relationships, which enable them to cooperate in matters of mutual interest, suggests that, eventually, all countries could overcome their differences.

These are great beginnings for being optimistic. It is good to be optimistic, as it makes the transition to world peace more convincing. No doubt that today we have the means, knowledge, and technology to make our world a peaceful, prosperous, and exciting place so that all can live in peace and harmony. Being optimistic means, we will become calm and united as members of one global family.

Peace analyst Hussain Danish asks several logical questions, including how this universal quest of humanity has been ignored for so long. Are we missing something? Could we do something different? And if so, what are they?

Here are a few thoughts:

- There is an element of mistrust among leaders and governments, not only from a military aspect but also in other areas, such as economic development projects. Leaders put self-interest and national self-interest before the requirements of the entire world. Every leader wants to grab a bigger piece of cake for their country. Therefore, this issue must be carefully examined and dealt with.

- Children must grow up and be educated with the principle of peace approach. Children are the best target group to understand the importance of lasting peace, and the best place to start is at home and school. Children must learn that people of other nations, religions and cultures are good and that there is only one race, the human race.

- They are removing extremes of wealth and poverty. Wealth and poverty extremes are severe obstacles to world peace and a universal problem today. It keeps the world in a state of instability.

The benefits

Peace increases the chance of development: A tranquil, peaceful society will decrease risks and volatility, increasing economic development opportunities and allowing long-term plans. Suppose nations at war or with internal conflicts had instead focused their efforts and resources towards improving the lives of their citizens. In that case, they too could have been among the leading developing and, in some instances, developed countries. During peace, resources will be allocated more efficiently, thus, maintaining global economic sustainability. This means protecting the Earth's resources to improve the life of this generation without upsetting those of future generations. Of course, laying the foundations for a truly peaceful society for the future generation, an age we have not met yet, is a big challenge, but it is worth doing.

Of course, creating peace is necessary, but more is needed for economic development. Developing countries have to deal with several other challenges. For example, in the last few decades, the economies of several developing countries have improved significantly. Relative peace and security in those countries have been responsible for their economic development. Other factors are also accountable, including increasing the enrolment of girls in primary and secondary schools, women empowerment, modernisation of agriculture with appropriate technology, development of microfinance, a decline in corruption, and relative improvement in governance. Although multinational corporations have several disadvantages, their positive role has provided employment opportunities for millions in developing countries.

We must distinguish between economic growth and development when discussing the economics of peace. Growth is a quantitative concept measured by Gross Domestic Product (GDP), which only considers the monetary value of goods and services produced within a specific time without paying much attention to the products made. For instance, if the production of military items increases, GDP counts them as a part of economic growth, even though these products negatively affect peace, the environment, well-being, and, more importantly, human lives. GDP does not consider such adverse effects known as negative externalities. However, development is referred to qualitative changes and their relationship with social, environmental, economic and spiritual aspects of life. It is concerned mainly with the quality of life and the long-term welfare of the community. Maintaining peace is one of the most critical factors contributing to the quality of life. Thus, economic development considers peacebuilding; economic growth overlooks it. Augusto Lopez-Claros and Daniel Perell states, "One of the most exciting developments in the constellation of recent proposals is related to developing indicators that move measurement beyond GDP."[23]

To imagine how important is the role of peace in a nation's economic performance, we can compare economic development and prosperity and the state of happiness of the citizens of peaceful countries with characteristics of life improvement and those with violence, tension and internal conflict. The result will be astonishing. In 2008, Joseph Stiglitz, Amartya Sen, and Jean-Paul Fitoussi considered better measures of happiness and social progress. They considered quality-of-life indicators, such as people's health, education, personal fulfilment, job satisfaction, and a community's environmental quality.

Waste of resources is uneconomical: Suppose we define economics, as stated by Alfred Marshall, as the study of humankind in the ordinary business of life. In that case, violence, conflict and aggression are not the usual way of life. Therefore, in theory, economists agree that peace is good and war is dreadful. Peace brings prosperity, and war leads to misery. In economics, resource waste is considered uneconomical, wrong, and costly to any economic activity. Waste of resources is an essential issue of concern in any economic textbook and denounces any actions that lead to wastage. During a war, a government increases its expenditures and burdens civilians.

During the war, resources are destroyed, which adds to the cost of production and increases the prices of goods and services. This, in return, creates shortages of essential products. As a result, both consumers and producers suffer greatly. In theory, economists are concerned about the cost of starting a new war – not just the cost to taxpayers but also the potential impact on the economy, oil prices, the stock market, inflation, unemployment, and living standards. Economists are also highly concerned about the opportunity cost of resources allocated to war, both human and monetary. Therefore, in theory, economists do not support violence of any kind.

There is an inherent 'opportunity cost' for governments' spending on war. Money that is spent in one area cannot be spent on another. A high military expenditure detracts from citizens' quality of life by limiting spending on developmental and social programs, a significant concern in developing countries. To explain this further, I will use a well-known economic model called the 'production possibility frontier.' Economists use this technique to demonstrate the efficient use of scarce resources over time. For example, at a time of war, if there is a need to increase the production of military items, we would have to give up some of the production of civilian goods and services such as education, health, and housing. This is because the additional production of military goods and services has an opportunity cost – in this case, social interests. In other words, the opportunity cost of producing extra units of military goods is the sacrifice of civilian goods.

Consequently, there is a trade-off between war and peace. Assigning a higher priority to stability requires a lower focus on war. As Muhammad Yunus (1998) states, "Putting more resources into improving the lives of the poor is a better strategy than spending it on guns." Therefore, there is less economic pressure on the life of people during peacetime.

Economic efficiency is that in peacetime: Another related factor closely linked with economic efficiency is that those goods and services that promote violence and are not in line with human dignity will be eliminated from the market. Some, however, may wonder what the replacement for the economic losses of such elimination will be. Undoubtedly, there will be opportunities to create alternative job prospects for producing goods and services that benefit human nobility. A country's achievements are numerous during peacetime, particularly with innovation, infrastructure, and human development. During peacetime, a government can spend all its resources to benefit its citizens.

Plans need to be in place to ensure that the use and transformations of resources are relatively peaceful and, at the same time, in coordination and conformity with an accountable and trustworthy source—peaceful means using resources now, keeping them safe for future generations, and protecting the ecosystem. By establishing truthfulness, trustworthiness, responsibility, and accountability, individuals and firms will ensure that resources are used most effectively and efficiently. Therefore, moral principles can shape economic attitudes and behaviour and bring a fundamental transformation in the life of people and institutions.

Some of the economic benefits of peace at a glance:

- Those goods and services promoting violence and not befitting human dignity will be eliminated with peace and an ideal world.
- With peace and considering human nobility, there will be opportunities to create alternative job prospects for producing goods and services that benefit human dignity.
- With peace, a government can allocate all its resources for the benefit of its citizens, particularly with innovation, infrastructure, and human development.
- With a tranquil, peaceful society, the economy will decrease risks and volatility, increasing opportunities to make long-term plans.
- Suppose nations at war or with internal conflicts had instead focused their efforts and resources towards improving the lives of their citizens. In that case, they too could have been among the leading developing and, in some instances, developed countries.

- A high level of military spending detracts from citizens' quality of life by limiting spending on developmental and social programs, a significant concern in developing countries.

- With peace, resources will be allocated more efficiently, resulting in maintaining global economic sustainability, which is protecting the Earth's resources for improving the life of this generation and future generations' lives.

- With peace, the benefits of globalisation will be distributed more fairly among world citizens.

- With peace, globalisation will work better for many people experiencing poverty. It will work better for much of the environment.

Family values as a symbol of peace

The family model can successfully make peace a norm, a way of life, and a cultural phenomenon in a global society. The best place to make peace a norm is in the family. The family unit represents the backbone of society. It comprises certain relationships between its members, coordinating human actions and harmonising planning processes. Looking at the characteristics and behaviour of a family in a time of decision-making, specific values are noted when behaving towards each other and those outside the family unit. Of course, the structure of a society is much more complex than a family unit. However, the view here is that these value principles, when effectively working within this unit of society, can become a cultural phenomenon and a way of life in the entire community. It is in the family that children learn about others. The concept of the enemy must disappear in the family model. We are all friends and not strangers.

Parents, schools, the community, and the government can be engaged in preparing children to grow up with respect, forgiveness, and friendliness. How can we have, for example, peace and stability in a region when children are raised in an environment of 'them and us' and 'hatred' and 'revenge'? Children should grow up with an understanding that there are no strangers and there are no enemies. Children should associate with all people with friendliness, fellowship, kindness, and forgiveness. A set of fundamental values common to all societies, such as love, respect, sacrifice, and trust. These core ethical values must be incorporated universally in all educational institutions and practised by all children. In this way, children grow up in a culture of praising and practising those moral principles necessary for creating authentic and lasting peace. Thus, values and virtues must become the norm and a part of the belief system. This subsequently will turn into a cultural phenomenon, which becomes exceptionally natural and easy to practice in the long run.

Schools can promote the concept of world citizenship. Promoting and understanding the concept of world citizenship helps eliminate all kinds of prejudices which cause conflict in many societies. As responsible world citizens, the earth's resources will be used more effectively and efficiently, leading to mutual trade, economic growth, job creation, and poverty reduction. World citizenship includes not only privileges but also responsibilities. It indicates that the problems and challenges have to be faced by all. To solve issues humanity faces, individuals and institutions should consider a holistic and multi-disciplinary approach.

Therefore, we have never been so capable of achieving world peace. The astounding progress that has taken place in the fields of communication, transportation, and information technology has provided many opportunities to increase the chances of achieving peace. Most importantly, it is the fact that a universally high consciousness exists of the horrors of war being experienced by millions of people throughout the world and the eminent dangers that await all of us if we do not find a way to co-exist on this beautiful planet peacefully.

Conclusion

This chapter will be concluded with a section from the Promise of World Peace, a statement by the International Governing Council of the Bahá'í Faith, the Universal House of Justice:

The Great Peace towards which people of good will throughout the centuries have inclined their hearts, of which seers and poets for countless generations have expressed their vision, and for which from age to age the sacred scriptures of mankind have constantly held the promise, is now at long last within the reach of the nations. For the first time in history, it is possible for everyone to view the entire planet, with all its myriad diversified peoples, in one perspective. World peace is not only possible but inevitable. It is the next stage in the evolution of this planet—in the words of one great thinker, "the planetization of mankind.

Whether peace is to be reached only after unimaginable horrors precipitated by humanity's stubborn clinging to old patterns of behaviour or is to be embraced now by an act of consultative will, is the choice before all who inhabit the earth. At this critical juncture, when the intractable problems confronting nations have been fused into one common concern for the whole world, failure to stem the tide of conflict and disorder would be unconscionably irresponsible.[24]

Chapter 8 -
The advent of new family life

Introduction

Family is the building block of society. Just as in a building where the foundation is the most crucial, the family is essential to developing the organisation of humanity. If the foundation of a building is weak, the entire building will be constructed on a fragile foundation and soon collapse. Therefore, to create a society, we need families. The question is: Why can't we make a society with individuals? Because family is the first step from individuality to communal life. The individual takes care of themself. Individual life is based on self-interest without considering the betterment of a larger unit. Society will not function appropriately based on individual life only.

Family from an economic perspective

The family is the smallest unit and central nucleus of society. The family consisting of parents and children constitute the fundamental unit of society and is the primary social institution or the first level of organisation. At this stage, the division of labour is formed and understood. As social institutions multiply and diversify, society becomes enlarged and complex, and its organisational form advances. This is the foundation of all human relationships; a love relationship produces life. Life leads to growth; growth manifests itself in development. Development demands change, and change cause progress.

The family's economy is based on family members' composition. The real success of the family as a living socio-economic unit is based on the fact that each enters into a covenant of love and care for the other. The integrity of the family is based on mutual love, trust, service, compassion and sacrifice. The family persists as long as the nature of love and care exists. The family's economy is thus dependent on the spiritual constitution of the family members. Therefore, we see the first logical connection between spirituality and economics. Defining family from an economic perspective, then several economic activities are possible and relevant directly or indirectly to the role of family, such as the creation of human, resource development of human capital, and social capital creation. In other words, the three main principles of production, distribution and consumption manifest themselves with family.

Most production is geared towards families, for they need to be provided with everything. Families need food, clothes, a house, vehicles, toys, and kitchen supplies. Families are consumers. Without consumers, the economy is unworkable; therefore, families are essential to the economy.

Consequently, investment in families is vital to have quality families. Early education and care are part of this investment strategy. It provides a three-part benefit to communities: It promotes young children's social, emotional, and intellectual development to be more successful in school. These children, later in life, become valuable employees for various firms. And it is a significant economic sector in its own right. Therefore, policymakers and local governments should focus more on the economic benefits of families with children.

Coming down to the practical level, what does this mean? Practically it means that the needs of an individual being many and varied, that is to say, unlimited, but, with our resources, capacity and efforts to satisfy those needs being limited, it becomes necessary that we enter into an agreement or covenant with others whereby we can concentrate all our resources of capacity, effort and time to produce some of the things which we and others can use, and against which we will be able to receive in exchange some of the goods and services which others will produce. This is what division of labour means, symmetry dependent on reciprocation. For this arrangement to become practicable and successful, it is necessary that there exist a certain amount of understanding and faith in each other; in other words, mutual trust that while I am doing this, you must do that; while you are giving me the right to expect the production of something from you, I am giving you the freedom to expect something from me, and this I consider is my duty. In other words, the fundamental economic relationship is one of reciprocal action, corresponding to the interdependent and reciprocating nature of human beings. The basis of this reciprocal action is an honest and sincere commitment to do as mutually agreed faithfully. Morality is the spirit that directs conduct to conform to conscience, thus, is the pivot of all economic reciprocal relationship leading to activities of production, distribution and consumption, whatever the level may be, between the members of the same family, between families, between communities, local, national or international.

Household Economic Management

One of the main areas in social sciences that entered the economic field is the institution of the family. The family is considered the first human institution and the foundation of many human behaviours and decision-making. Therefore, the family is prone to be able to study its evolution by entering into economic models. Based on this, the collection of works and efforts made by economists in this direction is called family economy or Household Economic Management. As the smallest unit that plays a role in the economy, the family plays the most crucial role. Apart from the direct effect that families have on the economy, all economic returns, even if indirectly, are ultimately spent on people who are members of a family. Therefore, the effect of the whole economy of families on the national economy and consequently on the world economy is very broad all-round. Thus, the role of the family in the overall economy can be considered.

The most crucial point in household economic management is undoubtedly achieving the correct consumption pattern (cost management) and establishing a suitable income system (income management). The family's financial management under normal conditions should be adjusted based on each family member's income and expenses. Like in the family, parents should apply emotional, psychological, and social management in discussing spending and creating a balance between income and expenses; management is also needed as another part.

Each family is considered a small economic enterprise that needs to manage resources.

To achieve a society with a flourishing economy, the role and duty of the family cannot be ignored. The family economy has two fundamental aspects: first, Income management through the earnings of family members eligible to work. Second, cost management, through achieving the correct consumption pattern. Sufficient efforts to achieve economic benefits can be accompanied by rational and ethical principles that make the family economy healthy and stable. The economic culture of families associated with how to produce, how to distribute and how much to consume in the family can play a significant role in the economic growth and development of the country. The family is society's only source of human resources and the most important and influential institution in directing and shaping people's economic behaviour.

To achieve a society with a flourishing economy, the role and duty of the family cannot be ignored. The family economy has two fundamental aspects: first, Income management through the earnings of family members eligible to work. Second, cost management, through achieving the correct consumption pattern. Sufficient efforts to achieve economic benefits can be accompanied by rational and ethical principles that make the family economy healthy and stable. The economic culture of families associated with how to produce, how to distribute and how much to consume in the family can play a significant role in the economic growth and development of the country. The family is society's only source of human resources and the most important and influential institution in directing and shaping people's economic behaviour.

Let's consider the topic of economics, defined as the study of human behaviour in the ordinary course of life, as stated by the well-known economist Alfred Marshall. It can be said that family economics is the science of home planning, managing the family's financial resources, and establishing a balance between income and expenditures. Therefore, what we mean by the family economy is the optimal allocation of the limited resources available to the family's needs, away from extravagance and wastage.

Since the family, as the smallest unit of society, is the principal place of life, we can say that the behaviour of family members influences the four economic principles of production, distribution, consumption, and the flow of money with an adequate education and the conduct of all members. Therefore, all employees and workers in the market are affected by the family culture. If families improve from the aspect of culture and behavioural patterns towards economic affairs, in that case, the country's culture of work and productivity will be enhanced. Productivity is the proper and effective use of each of the production factors. Increasing productivity is related to four basic principles of economics: production, distribution, consumption and the flow of money, and they all start with the members of the family unit.

The effect of the family through education is divided into two main parts: The impact of material teachings and the development of spiritual and moral teachings.

Material teachings are necessary for the material aspects of human life, such as reading and writing, natural sciences and mathematics, and human sciences, including economics.

The family unit lives in an open society and is not isolated. Thus, families have relationships with others. The comfort of the family unit depends on the well-being of the neighbours and many more families in the community. This is important because the spiritual principle of compassion effectively works within this unit of society. The family becomes much more sensitive and understanding when they realise that their comfort and well-being are dependent on the well-being and comfort of others. Applying the principle of compassion to the wider society means having a preference for the happiness of others. It is to look after our personal and family satisfaction without forgetting our empathy towards others in society. Thus, self-interest and the selfish quality of greed must be replaced by the selfless quality of compassion. Of course, this is a big challenge for an individual and the family unit. However, it can be achieved in the long run by educating children in understanding the concept of 'world citizenship'.

Family unit as a role model

The family unit offers an ideal setting shaped by those moral attributes contributing to an appropriate view of economics in transition. A few examples are helpful: The partnership is one of the features of the family model. This approach is based on an explicit model of the caring and helping process. It demonstrates how a partnership enables parents and children to overcome difficulties effectively and fulfil their goals. The relationship of the family members is based on mutual love, trust and sacrifices for one another. These qualities are essential for the family to succeed; otherwise, the family will become dysfunctional and chaotic and break apart. A family can function with these moral and spiritual principles even with limited resources. Also, in the family unit, the division of labour applies too, where each member has a different but complementary function. Therefore, the family analogy is the pivot of all economic reciprocal relationships leading to activities of production, distribution and consumption, the three fundamental principles of modern economics. This is where we see a logical connection between moral principles and economics. Of course, the structure of contemporary family and economics is much more complex, with various functions.

Within a community, much importance should be placed on strengthening the concept of family and its relationship with those outside the family unit. Moral education and a better understanding of the significance of marriage and family life helped pave the way. Virtuous principles define the relationship between an individual and the whole society. As a result, those values become essential to the individual and the community's life. Thus, it becomes natural for a person to respect and care for fellow human beings and the creation of a new generation.

Looking at the similarities of the family unit and its relationship with the larger society and those beautiful principles that work within a family, we should ask why such attractive principles are not working in the broader community. For example, in a family unit with minimal resources, the weaker members of the family, mostly children, are under extreme care. How come, in the broader society, over a billion people in the world are hungry? In the family unit, the members share resources based on equity. How come in the broader society, eighty per cent of the world's resources are in the hands of twenty per cent of the population, and the gap is increasing? In the family unit, most activities are based on cooperation. How come, in the broader society, it is based on aggressive competition? And in the family unit, members sacrifice their well-being so that other family members are better off. Still, in the broader society, it is based on self-interest and, even worse, selfishness. In the larger community, our undertakings and behaviours seem to be based on models and systems that are in place and mostly obsolete.

How can a wider society benefit by having strong and self-sufficient families? All type of protection is provided by government or private institutions. Regarding safety, the government provides significant social welfare today, and many people depend on government funds. In the past, children were the asset of a home. Today, they are more luxurious. They go as their education finishes, and it is time for them to return some money. Therefore, government or private institutions outside the family provide all types of protection. A family can't deal with their problems without outside help.

Regarding the issue of the family and its function in the wider society, it is essential to consider that most people are altruistic and have a certain level of compassion and understanding to help others. For example, to form a family, couples reach an agreement or covenant with each other, focusing their energies on being loyal to each other and supporting each other and their children. The same thing is true about the human family. A strong family structure can offer companionship, support, security, understanding, advice, comfort, harmony, and help in times of crisis. We use all our resources to produce goods and services that benefit all members through a justified exchange mechanism based on altruistic nature. A strong family structure can offer companionship, support, security, understanding, advice, comfort, harmony, and help in times of crisis. However, the characteristics and functioning of today's family are complex and may be challenging to use as a symbol for contemporary economic issues. Applying the family metaphor is more practical in small communities and small-scale operations.

As family is a role model for the wider society, parents are a role model for children at home. Children at home follow their parents willingly or unwillingly. So, parents are the role model for children. Economic relations at home are one of the most important relations in the family, and this will also impact the larger society. The feeling of closeness between the economic relations at home will have an effect outside of the house. Therefore, a successful household manager thinks about improving relations and the best use of what is available at home. Other sources of information, including some ideas about supply and demand, prices, inflation, unemployment, tax laws, discounts, savings, and interest rates, contribute significantly to household management, affecting the overall economy similarly.

For several reasons, family formation is suitable for its own sake and society's benefits, including:

- The government provides all kinds of help and support for families, such as a special family welfare fund, a special fund for children's welfare, use for work and employment, and special laws for paying taxes fairly.
- Ethics-related courses have been removed from many public schools in the countries; in this case, the vital task is the responsibility of the families. The

role of parents in the education of moral values such as honesty, trustworthiness and truthfulness, cooperation and service and other moral virtues are significant, and children should grow up with moral virtues to deal with a life comprising both spiritual and material magnitudes in the long run.

- The family is the source and basis of social work and employment. Without the family, the labour market and the entire economy of society will go into stagnation and unproductivity.

- Advanced families can create more security, prosperity, hope, unity, and societal stability in economic and social crises.

The importance of the role of the family can be summarised in a few points:
- In the role of preparation and economical procurement
- In the role of protection and security of people
- In the part of the education of family members and thus the whole society
- In the position of moral and emotional support for people

Economic advantages of family structure

- Specialisation and exchange: Family members can specialise; and the whole community will benefit from different services through the business.

- Economies of scale: Housing for two people costs less than one. Or it takes less time to prepare meals for two people than it does to prepare for one.

- Public goods: A public good has the characteristic that the consumption of the item by one person does not diminish the amount available for consumption by others, for example, watching a movie. In this case, the amount of consumption and satisfaction an individual obtains from the film is probably not reduced if another person watches it too.

- Externalities in consumption: When two people care for one another, one partner may derive satisfaction from the enjoyment and happiness of the other.

- Family investment: Opportunity for family-specific investments refers to the development of skills, knowledge, and other items worth more in a family than the absence of family. The prime example is the raising of children. Children provide their parents with considerable satisfaction.

- Risk pooling: If one spouse becomes unemployed, the couple can rely on the other spouse to cover at least part of the household expenses.

- Institutional benefits: Including coverage by a spouse's health insurance, pension, Social Security benefits, and in some countries, child allowance.

Minimum standards of living for a family

In a general view, poverty indicates how much a typical family lacks the money to buy the necessities of life. Many poverty indicators are defined based on income levels, while poverty in its broadest sense is more than not having money. Poverty can be considered based on having the necessities of life - such as housing or food - access to welfare-enhancing services - such as transportation, education, and health - and the ability to participate in decisions that shape the individual's and society's future. In another grouping, poverty can be defined in absolute and relative terms.

Measuring family income or expenses as the ability of the family to purchase the required goods and services is a direct method of measuring poverty and welfare in society. For this measurement, indirect methods or measuring the manifestations of poverty can also be used. From this perspective, poverty is viewed as a multidimensional phenomenon and a poor family is considered to be deprived of the signs of normal life. For example, if a family cannot send its children to school or lives in an inappropriate place, uses unsanitary water, and does not have access to basic necessities such as refrigerators and electricity, it is considered poor. The calculation of the multidimensional poverty index, in which education, health, housing, family assets, and the level and stability of income are considered, shows that poverty in Iranian families is from the perspective of deprivation of education, health, and living conditions, which the United Nations Development Program considers in comparing countries. These families can be regarded as poor.

The place of children in economics

It is the general understanding that the subject of economics is for the university level and for the top managers of large organisations to know. Although this is an acceptable point, the place of economics is at home. For the day-to-day understanding of the market and issues related to daily news, children and parents should be acquainted with some of the principles of economics.

In the family model, children have an important place in the economy. They are considered the economic capital of a community. Children must know the role and purpose of economics and the market, which is about tools available to use wisely for improving the standard of communities. It will be educational and interesting to children to know the answer to questions such as: Why should we work? Why should we save some of our money? Why should we care for the environment? And the relationship between income and expenditure. Children should know about good and bad costs and expenditures and why bad costs are affecting the environment severely. Also, understanding the function of money, whether money brings happiness, what happiness is, and most importantly, knowing the purpose of life. The response to these questions and many other economic issues that we are dealing with on daily can be found at home as parents and children learn together. These are the same issues and topics used in the largest and most prominent commercial organisations and also in academia.

In a family setting, children learn the proper decision-making method through the principle of consultation. In planning, family members set goals for themselves to achieve. The consultation principle helps the family carry out an effective planning process. Children learn the importance of compassion, an inner quality and a duty binding the individual to prefer others. Consultation, on the other hand, is an outward action and right of the individual to self-expression. The method of consultation provides an opportunity for each member to contribute to accomplishing the goals. This, in return, influences the relationship and subsequently improves the behaviour of individual family members. These concepts that are discussed in the family environment have a significant effect on the broader community. Children and teenagers will soon be managers and policymakers in the private and public sectors. Family consultation inspires them to make the right judgements and right decisions for the economic well-being of the communities.

The economic crisis affects children and their families profoundly. It has ripple effects in many areas where children and youth are placed. Stressful factors such as lowering the quality of life, including food and clothing, are primarily due to parents' unemployment, and children still need to become familiar with such a phenomenon. Therefore, it is essential to clarify for children the importance of work and the issue of unemployment and its consequences in the family.

Losing a job also causes the loss of family savings, and children should be aware of it and be conscious of its cause. In low-income families, basic needs such as food security, health care, and shelter may be more pressing. High poverty rates are associated with increased family economic crises such as child neglect and abuse. More broadly, a worsening economy can affect the budgets of public schools and community health centres, which are stretched when children, youth and families need their services most. Children and teenagers are especially vulnerable because they undergo critical developmental changes. Economic stress often causes problems in terms of anxiety, low self-esteem and other emotional and behavioural issues. Therefore, in times of economic crisis, parents should talk to their children about financial uncertainties and fears. Rising inflation stresses many families, but age-appropriate discussions about financial concerns can help ease anxiety among children. For example, explaining to children how the economy affects employment and job opportunities can give them a better idea of what is happening in the market. Therefore, an economy managed and executed by the family positively affects the whole society, of which the economy is a part.

The importance of saving

Savings not only plays a vital role in the economy of families but also play a fundamental role in the economy of a country. The definition of savings is an increase in net wealth or unspent income. With these definitions, storing money in a healthy savings account is helpful in a period of uncertain financial conditions. No one wants to be stressed because they know they might run out of money later in life. Many examples of people who need more money due to job loss, disability, illness, education, etc. Therefore, from a purely economic point of view, a factor that significantly impacts the measure of happiness, in the long run, is the amount of savings. Unfortunately, in poorer families where the income level is low, the level of saving is not enough. Most of the income is spent on essential products in such families, and little is left for savings. Saving is a necessary source of wealth in the long run. People can buy a house for themselves and enjoy a better life as a result. Saving also helps older people to enjoy a happier life during retirement. There may come a time when some governments will only be able to support retirees for a short time. In this case, savings will make this group comfortable in their old age. It can be said that saving increases happiness. People who set their future goals by saving money or planning for themselves always feel happier than ordinary people because they have provided a way of security and a sense of well-being and strengthened themselves as a whole.

Tackling an economic crisis

A crisis of any kind cannot be predicted or welcomed. The crisis period is very worrying and causes stress for all family members. If family members are experiencing stress and tension during an economic crisis, here are some practical ways to help create more comfort and reduce anxiety and maintain the mental health of the family and its effects:

- Families should look at their finances and decide if they need to make major or minor changes to improve the budget. It is essential to evaluate each situation individually. Family regular budget reviews are great ways to communicate frequently.
- Determining goals should be an essential part of family consultation. It is vital to prioritise short-term and long-term goals and decide on the resources needed to support each plan.
- Working together is fun for families and produces actual results. Couples should work together to set priorities, even if one person is more financially involved in the day-to-day budget than the other.

- Regular and planned communication between all family members helps to reduce stress by creating different and foreseeable preparations. For example, when children participate in consultation and decision-making, they feel less worried. Hence, sharing power, allowing children to make age-appropriate choices, and helping the family reduce worry and anxiety. One suggestion is to let children be in charge of minor expenses at home with a simple budgeting plan.

- One of the sources of stress is media news, especially if it needs to be presented with accuracy, wrong figures and data, or misinterpretation by incompetent people. So, if all the bad news about the economy is causing stress, it's best to ignore it for a while. It is essential to get your information from reliable sources.

- Worrying about things outside our control, such as the macroeconomy, is not appropriate or productive. The government should be responsible and concerned about macroeconomic goals such as unemployment, inflation, economic growth and international trade. We should do more things related to the microeconomy and help improve the situation at the individual and family levels. In this way, we can indirectly help the macroeconomic part as well.

- Thoughts have substantial effects on how we think and feel. Hence, it is essential to keep our thoughts optimistic. Positive thinking can help reduce the impact of worry on the body and mind.

- Numerous things enrich life, and most are unrelated to money. We must focus on togetherness, creativity, peace, and spirituality to take some of our attention away from the economic situation. It is also important for families to take care of themselves all the time, not just in times of crisis.

- We must know our fear and anxiety and find ways to eliminate them. Children learn and react by watching others. Let's remember that our worries cause children to worry more. Therefore, showing them healthy ways to manage these feelings is necessary. It is important for families not to let fear into them. There are solutions to the most complex financial problems, even if they seem far away. Reduce your anxiety through family activities. Note that your depression also spreads to family members.

- In times of crisis, connecting with our loved ones is important. Contact friends and family and support them. We can reduce our worries by talking to our close friends. Our friends do not need to be experts in the field of depression. They need to be good listeners. Also, anxiety can be reduced with social and altruistic and voluntary activities.

Family Love Account

It was established that the family constitutes the most fundamental unit of society and is the primary social institution. As social institutions multiply and diversify, society becomes enlarged and complex, and its organisational form advances. Without family, there will be no community, nation, or civilisation. Family plays a vital role in fulfilling individuals' emotional and physical needs. These parts are needed for achieving economic and social development.

Opening a 'family love account' is recommended here to all families. This account is not a physical or financial account. However, in a way, it helps the holders of this account become materially and emotionally better off.

Ingredients for the Family Love Account

Love

Love is the first ingredient to be deposited into this non-financial saving account. We assume that the couple getting married has already started this process and deposited lots of it into this account. Love is an essential part of marriage. The good thing about this ingredient is that others can deposit into this account, such as parents and friends. Therefore, the account should be open to all. When there is so much love in this account, the couple wants to share some of it with others. Everyone must deposit into this account by acting on love. Now in what way does this account become richer or poorer? The Family Love Account becomes weaker or stronger depending on how the love factor function between the couple or the whole family. If we withdraw more and more from the account, it becomes poorer, and if more is deposited, the account becomes richer. Therefore, the family love account becomes stronger if we give our love continuously.

The relationship between family members must be loving, supportive, and unconditional love. It is the act of loving, a verb, and requires action. The feeling of loving depends on the activity in it. If there is no love, there won't be a feeling of love one day. To become stronger in love is to act upon it.

Consequently, love being a verb is possible when it is genuinely performed. In a strong family, love is acted on continuously. In a larger society, love is the foundation of all human relationships.

The covenant

The covenant is the second ingredient to be deposited into the Family Love Account. This is what is made between a couple. It is a commitment strongly connected with the first one, love. Covenant makes the account so strong that it becomes a model for others to open a similar account. With love and covenant, the couple makes the most crucial decision: each chooses to live with one person for the rest of their life.

Trust

The third essential ingredient of the Family Love Account is building and rebuilding a trust that should be respected forever. Therefore, the real success of the family as a living socio-economic unit is because each enters a covenant of mutual trust.

Cooperation

The fourth ingredient in this account is cooperation. In the marriage institution, we don't compete with each other. We cooperate. The analogy of the bird with two wings applies here. Man and woman are the two wings of a bird. Both men and women must be strong to fly higher and higher. They should not let the other wing become weak. They should always make each other stronger. Marriage is not a competition; the man and the woman should fly together. Cooperation is an essential part of a partnership and is one of the features of the family model. This approach is based on an explicit model of the caring and helping process. It demonstrates how a partnership enables parents and children to overcome difficulties, build strengths and resilience and fulfil their goals more effectively.

Consultation

The last suggested item to be deposited into the Family Love Account is the principle of loving consultation. This is a challenge. Consultation is not practised in many families. In other words, not enough was deposited into the Family Love Account. The absence of it will weaken the Family Love Account. Effective consultancy skills provide a way of facilitating change without taking control of it. Learning how to do this is vital for all members looking for a quality life. Considering that consultation is an art, some people take longer to understand and practice. We should keep our Family Love Account strong because of essential principles. A loving consultation keeps the couple united, and the Family Love Account becomes richer.

Conclusion

These principles form the backbone of a healthy family relationship. Certain principles govern relationships and are universal. A family is bound together with love, covenant, trust, cooperation, and consultation. And deviating from these principles brings unhappiness to families. By using these principles increasingly, the Family Love Account becomes richer and more prosperous.

Chapter 9 -
Women's empowerment - In the quest for gender equality

Introduction

To begin this subject, I like to mention two incidents, both of which are related to Bangladesh. The first event is cited in the book 'Ending Poverty' by Jeffrey Sachs[25], he writes:

> On one visit to Bangladesh, I picked up an English language morning newspaper, where I found an extensive insert of interviews with young women working in the garment sector. These stories were poignant, fascinating, and eye-opening. One by one, they recounted their arduous hours, the lack of Labour rights, and the harassment. What was most striking and unexpected about the stories was the repeated affirmation that this work was the greatest opportunity these women could ever have imagined and that their employment had changed their lives for the better.[26]

The second incident is my own experience. In the 1980s, the government of Bangladesh was of the opinion that the country's number one problem was population. As a student of economics, I was pondering how come the most important resource of an economy in a country is considered a problem. The United Nations used to help the government of Bangladesh financially to reduce population growth from 3% to 2.8% but failed. All the efforts done by the government and various international non-profit organisations did not significantly reduce the population growth.

On the other hand, religious beliefs prevented the solutions to reduce population growth. The view was that such control was against religious guidelines, and families were told they could have any number of children because God provided them with food. So, is population a problem, and in what sense?

Both incidents show that women are still deprived of the same opportunities and equality in decision-making as men and have yet to obtain their rights. The first incident didn't provide the equal opportunity to earn a wage equal to their male partners. In the second incident, they are not given the opportunity to make their own decision about how to live and how many children they want.

In this chapter, an analysis will be made of the importance of girls' education and the role of women in social, political, and economic development. Also, several practical ideas will be presented to reduce the wage gap between men and women.

With the increase in the enrolment of girls in schools and notably higher education in Bangladesh, we see significant positive changes affecting population control. For example, because of the rise in the rate of literate girls, the marriage age of girls increased. As a result, the number of children born to these girls decreased, and the population growth rate reduced significantly. Due to this decrease in the population growth rate, currently, this country can provide better living conditions for its people. Today, Bangladeshi families have more balanced economic conditions than families with a large population in the past and enjoy relative prosperity. Also, the education of the girls of this country has made them considered a workforce more than before. With improvement in education, along with technological advancement and increased know-how, this nation has made significant social and economic development. This exceptional achievement is attributed to the increasing enrolment of girls from primary schools to higher education. Thanks to the government of Bangladesh, private institutions, including the Grameen Bank founded by Mohammad Yunus, and more than anything else, the female population who were the cause of women empowerment.

Women's educational empowerment

Access to education is a fundamental aspect of women's empowerment. The presence of women in the enrolment rate, literacy level and gender equality has made significant progress. Despite the various obstacles for women to enter an educational environment, today, they manage to make up the majority of university attendees and perform better than their peers in university entrance exams as well as in graduation rates. The enrolment rate of women in schools and universities has been steadily increasing for many years. In fact, now the number of women in the universities of a number of countries such as Iran is more than men, who make up the majority of students. Women have made significant advances in academic achievement. Women's achievements are in many areas, including medical and health sciences, research and publications, academic leadership and international recognition. All these achievements have empowered women and contributed to the overall progress and development of those countries that have provided freedom, opportunities and means for progress. Women's scientific achievements inspire future generations and show the potential of women's participation in society through education and research.

Women's economic empowerment

Increasing women's labour force participation has contributed to any country's economic growth and social transformation. If women are seen as an active force, they will greatly impact the development and increase of the human capital of that society in terms of quality and quantity. Increasing women's participation in the workforce has positive effects on the economy and society. It helps to increase productivity, expand talent and increase economic growth. Women's economic empowerment also improves their social status, decision-making power and overall well-being. While women in some countries have traditionally been involved in educational, health care and administrative roles, their participation has expanded in other fields such as engineering, technology, financial sectors and entrepreneurship. The increasing presence of women in these sectors shows their growing abilities and aspirations. Women's entrepreneurship and leadership in business are significant. Women have embraced entrepreneurship and assumed leadership roles in various business sectors. Women-led businesses have significantly contributed to the overall economy, bringing about positive impacts and transformative changes.

One of the problems seems to be that women are considered the weaker gender in some societies, and their growth and development are given secondary priority. This way of thinking can be seen in the root of a society that first, all men should have the opportunity to work and earn money, then women should be allowed to participate in social, political and economic activities. They believe that because men are the head of the family, women's economic participation is considered a big obstacle to their employment and increases their unemployment level. Or sometimes, men do not allow their wives to work outside the home, which can be due to the male-controlled culture in many ways, in such a way that men have the right to property in several ways, including economic, sexual, and emotional. They are considered the property of husbands. It can be said that in such a culture, if women work, they are considered a threat to men's power and ownership, and for this reason, they are deprived of social and economic participation. The result of such thoughts and limitations is the low participation rate of women.

In economics, development is a discussion about expanding the infrastructure to improve market activities to welcome everyone into the economy. Economic development is not the end but a process that a country and its members take to reach a higher and more efficient level of economy. Achieving such a concept requires many factors that all work together to make the country achieve economic development.

In today's world, justice is used in different fields, and the reason is that resources are not distributed fairly, and to achieve a fair life, it is necessary to have a balanced level of activities that help economic growth and development. Regardless of this issue, humans need justice to pursue a sense of purposefulness and usefulness. We cannot demand economic development in a country. At the same time, we have not allowed a group of people in society to grow, fully enjoy or use the facilities and resources of that society equally. We must note that for any development purpose, the observance of justice as a fundamental economic concept is undeniable.

A large group of women around the world have yet to be exposed to serving society. A society will grow and prosper very quickly when it gives women skills for empowerment opportunities. A large part of a community's economic development can be seen in the presence of women in occupations and jobs that men have monopolised for years, and women did not play much of a role in it.

When society is on the path of development and growth and has the policy to use the presence of women, it must provide conditions for women to have a smooth process in the direction of moving in the path of development. This includes opportunities in education, science, politics, economics, and more. For example, to give women interested in economic and social fields the opportunity to acquire knowledge, to provide women who are mothers a position and space to work and do her duty as a mother, and with the education it promotes in society.

Dimensions of empowering women can be analysed in two parts, individual and collective. Individually, women should make much effort to compensate for injustices committed against them. Also, the self-confidence lost in this group of people in society must be restored. So that women have faith and confidence in themselves and their abilities and know that they have the capability and skills to work and play an influential role in society.

Women's empowerment can also continue from individual performance to social performance. This requires opportunities provided for women to enable them to serve communities, for example, in situations where women can have higher education and secure jobs. Many vocabularies that are associated with women must be removed permanently. I am talking about phrases such as: "A woman's place is in the kitchen, not at work", "A woman should be a child bearer only", and "The work environment is not safe for women". In a society that demands economic growth, the participation of women is undeniable.

Equal rights and opportunities for women and men

A bird symbol conveys the principle of equal rights for men and women. In a bird, both wings must be strong to fly well. If one wing is damaged or weak, it spins in the air until its head gets dizzy and falls. Our society today has the same problem. Equal opportunities have yet to be created in different parts of society. Equal opportunities in education and training, opportunities for prosperity and comfort, political, economic, and social conditions, and opportunities for women to acquire education, skills, talents, and decision-making. That is why our society is moving with one wing. And those with essential responsibilities in planning need help with implementation, knocking on every door, and need help finding a way. We must acknowledge that half of the world's population are women. It doesn't matter if someone is a woman or a man to acquire skills, talents, abilities, and qualifications.

Traditionally, it is frequently the case that women are relatively more productive in the home, and men are somewhat more effective in the market. This can be true because men and women are traditionally raised with different expectations and receive further education and training. It may also be the case that women are discriminated against in the labour market and that discrimination lowers their market earnings. Moreover, the traditional division of labour will likely magnify differences in men's and women's household and market skills because both types of mastery tend to increase with experience.

There is ample evidence that educational discrimination against women reinforces social inequality and hinders economic development. Closing the educational gender gap by expanding educational opportunities for women is economically desirable. It increases their productivity and results in greater labour force participation. It improves child health and nutrition, as more educated mothers lead to an increase in the quality of a nation's human resources. Because women carry a disproportionate burden of poverty, any significant improvements in their role and status via education can substantially break the vicious circle of poverty.

Most nations have recognised the importance of the equality of women and men in the social and economic equation. There is an emphasis on the participation of women in all aspects of community life. Women in the past did not have the opportunity to participate in the affairs of society. A woman's lack of progress and proficiency has been due to her need for equal education and opportunity. Had she been allowed this equality, there is no doubt she would be the counterpart of man in ability and capacity.

Let us express the concept of equal opportunities between men and women in another way. We, humans, have two hands, and we depend on both. Now, one hand is usually more substantial than the other. In some people, the right hand is more significant; in others, the left is. But the weaker hand still does much work. Many tasks require both hands. Do you know someone who has removed one hand because he is a little more vulnerable? Both hands should be given enough time and opportunity to do their job with the human body. It is only in this way that humans can achieve their goals. By cooperating with different parts of the human body, including both hands, humans can perform their activities for the best benefit. The human body is an excellent example of unity in diversity. That is, although each member of the human body has a separate task and does a different job, only when they work together with cooperation and unity balance is created in the human body, and that is when progress in any field is possible. How is it possible for the unity of humankind to occur without considering the entire humanity? How is it possible to have an economic balance in the world without the presence of half of the world's population who have extraordinary abilities and talents?

Importance of girls' education

Regarding the second incident mentioned earlier, in the last few decades, the public and private sectors in Bangladesh have made extensive investments in education, especially for girls, at all levels, from elementary to university. Therefore, today a significant percentage of girls are in universities and have higher education. This program caused the population growth in this country to decrease significantly, and the female population and their families enjoyed relative well-being.

Development experts Michael Todaro and Stephen Smith raise a reasonable and legitimate question: Why is girls' education important? Much empirical evidence shows that educational discrimination against women reinforces social inequality and delays economic development. Todaro and Smith's research in this field indicates that reducing the gender gap in education by expanding educational opportunities for girls will be economically desirable for several reasons:

- It increases their agriculture and factory productivity and results in more labour force participation.

- It improves children's health and nutrition because educated mothers pay more attention to the quality of human resources for future generations.

- Since women bear a disproportionate share of the burden of poverty, any significant improvement in their role and position through education can substantially break the vicious cycle of poverty.

Benefits of girl's education

The immediate benefits and long-term impact of educating girls are remarkable. In this section, several advantages are mentioned:

- When girls are educated, health improves, economies grow, societies transform, and families and their communities and nations flourish. In other words, educated girls change the world.

- An educated girl can increase her income and improve her living conditions. More income means better nutrition and health care for himself and her family. Income can be a motivation to get out of the cycle of poverty. She also has the right to choose and has more job opportunities in life.

- An educated girl breaks the cultural pattern of marrying girls off as children. Girls with a higher level of education are also less likely to have children at a young age (UNESCO). Marrying later means that when she becomes a mother, she will not be a child herself and will have better mental and spiritual maturity, and as a result, will help raise children.

- Educated mother has better knowledge about pregnancy prevention. An educated mother may have fewer children and provide better care at home, thus increasing the value of her children's human capital.

- Educated mothers die less during childbirth. Educated women's knowledge of health care helps reduce maternal mortality during pregnancy, birth, and postpartum. Increasing girls' education also leads to more excellent assistance from women's health care providers in prenatal and follow-up care and can save the lives of women and babies.

- Educated mothers have healthier children. The most significant factor in reducing the death rate among children under five is more education for women. More education helps women make better decisions about prenatal care, basic hygiene, nutrition, and immunisation, all of which contribute to healthier children.

- Children of educated mothers are less malnourished. An educated mother is more likely to feed her children healthy food, recognise the signs of malnutrition, and act if a problem is suspected. Proper nutrition in a young child helps the normal development of the brain and body and better health and well-being.

- An educated woman invests in future generations and her community. An educated woman affects the way her children are raised, and it also affects her role in the family and society. An educated mother is more than twice as likely to send her children to school, thus perpetuating the education cycle and setting an example for future generations.

- Educated women experience less discrimination. Educated girls and young women are more aware of their rights. They are more likely to defend themselves and their children in male-dominated cultures.

- Educated girls and women have more self-confidence and freedom in making decisions that affect their lives. They are better equipped to challenge women's cultural imperatives, such as raising children and doing housework. Education empowers young women to think beyond cultural norms and pursue their dreams for a better life.

- Proper education protects women from abuse. Extremists, especially religious extremists, know that intelligent girls are less oppressed. Educating girls protects against domestic violence, rape, and child marriage. Each additional year of schooling is associated with a one per cent increase in women's ability to refuse sex with their partners.

- Women with secondary education are less at risk of violence than women without education. Educated women are more likely to work outside the home, avoid isolation, and earn and be financially independent, reducing their vulnerability to domestic and physical abuse.

In many cultures, when the family's income is small, practically a significant amount of the women's income is used to feed the family. Since this amount is significantly lower for men, an increase in men's income leads to less than the proportional amount in what is available in the budget to provide daily needs. Thus, it is not surprising that programs designed to improve nutrition and family health are more effective when they target women than when they target men.

Consequently, incredible things happen when a girl gets the education she needs. Her life improves; she has confidence, earns money, helps the economy, and sets the example of self-determination for the girls and women of their community. We all know that educating girls is important. There is no doubt about it. Therefore, investing in girls' education must be allowed. Girls' education is the most critical determinant of progress for sustainable development, from mortality reduction to economic growth, democracy, equality, and human rights. Therefore, investing more in the education of girls has excellent monetary value.

However, there are challenges ahead that we must remember, not only in getting girls to access education but also in the types of subjects in school and learning, as well as ensuring that education equips them for the future and has an impact. Also, the opportunities to invest in girls' education will make life flourish for themselves and bring widespread economic and social benefits to all.

UNESCO has researched the benefits of investing in girls' education:

- The benefits of investing in girls' education are significant. An educated girl is likely to increase her earning potential and reduce poverty in her community. Such effects are passed from generation to generation. Educated girls have healthier and more educated children.

- Improving literacy can have a significant impact on women's income. In Pakistan, working women with high literacy skills earned 95% more than women with poor or no literacy skills. Educated women invest 90% of their income in playing a more significant economic role in their families and communities.

- Investing in girls' education also helps delay early marriage and parenthood. If all girls in sub-Saharan Africa and South and West Asia had a secondary education, child marriage would drop by 64 per cent.

- At a broader societal level, more educated girls lead to more female leaders, lower levels of population growth, and subsequent reductions in climate change pressures. The power of girls' education in developing the national economy is undeniable.

UNESCO's investment approach in girls' education is of three types:

i.   We work with governments to strengthen policies and laws that support and protect girls, including from school violence.

ii.   We support providing educational opportunities for vulnerable girls, including through scholarships, cash transfers, gender-sensitive curricula and teacher training.

iii.   We support girls' education locally, nationally, and globally.

Therefore, investing in girls' education is right for economic and social development.

Closing the wage gap

Realising equal opportunities for men and women is an essential factor in correcting the failure and weakness of the labour market, including removing obstacles to increasing production. In studying the global gender gap, it is necessary to improve women's conditions in five areas: economic opportunity, economic participation, political empowerment, access to education, and health and well-being.

Helena Trachsel, the former heads of the Gender Equality Office in Zurich, has proposed six practical theories for closing the gender pay gap, as follows:

i. During the interview, questions such as what salary level you offer for yourself should be removed because usually, women provide a lower salary for themselves to be selected.

ii. The education of equal rights of men and women should be included in the training of institutional workers. Especially such activity should be considered permanently for the youth.

iii. Institutions should clearly announce that women's employment is part of their permanent plan.

iv. The promotion and rights of all employees, men and women, should be constantly monitored and evaluated, and appropriate solutions should be considered to improve it.

v. Work should be flexible, especially for mothers who can work from home or work part-time.

vi. Companies should try to hire 50/50 male and female employees. The same procedure should be done in all parts of the organisation, especially management.

Conclusion

Education opportunities and positive achievements provide the conditions for a significant transition to a meaningful standard of life. Half of the world's population, that is, women, as an essential part of the wealth of nations, have been neglected for a long time. Wealth can be multiplied through women's empowerment and, as a result, increasing the capacity of existing human resources. In modern times, countries compete to reduce the wage gap between men and women. The belief in equal opportunities for women and men is recognised as an ideal transition in social and economic participation. But still, much must be done. This principle has important implications in increasing labour supply and, thus, the production level. The benefits of discovering and using women's talent affect the whole of society. These include growing economic growth, especially in developing countries, and reducing the number of people living in poverty. The principle of equal opportunity for women and men will significantly enable the other half of the human population, women, to be empowered and enter social, political and economic activities at all levels.

Chapter 10 -
Investment in education as a top priority

Introduction

Extensive research has been done that human capital is the most valuable resource for a company now and in the future knowledge-based economy. To have a viable business, the employer requires those who do the work to produce an appropriate and effective performance, which significantly comes from employees. The efforts and activities of employees are the basis of competitive advantage for a business. We may argue that Factors of production, such as capital and natural resources, are inactive; if they are left to themselves, nothing will happen. Human resources are the active elements that gather wealth, exploit natural resources, establish social and political organisations, produce goods and services, and carry out innovations and other development activities. Any economy in transition will benefit immensely from adequate schooling with characteristics of intellectual and moral education.

Investment in education as a top priority

There is a growing recognition that investment in people is the key to development, and it influences increasing the wealth of a nation and poverty alleviation. Education, apart from affecting the national income, provides other opportunities for society. Expert in economic development, Michael Todaro, discusses several opportunities that investment in education can offer to increase the wealth of a nation through economic development, including creating a more productive labour force and endowing it with advanced knowledge and skills, providing widespread employment and income-earning opportunities for all kinds of jobs, creating a class of educated leaders in government services and private and public corporations, and providing the type of training and education that would promote literacy and essential skills for affecting 'human capital'. In particular, the economic returns from extra investment in teaching the lower-income group in developing countries will be substantial. The positive opportunities and accomplishments achieved through education will create the conditions for a smoother process of attaining a meaningful standard of living.

Today's market has recognised the necessity of investment in education and training as a prerequisite for increasing productivity and profitability. The World Bank has done a comprehensive study, which shows that investing more in education and training directly impacts economic performance and multiplying the wealth of a nation. The findings show that the profitability of investment in education is an attractive opportunity, particularly in developing countries.[27] Of course, the economic returns from extra investment in education can vary according to the stage of economic development a country has achieved, the amount invested in training and education, and the type of education required in the labour market, which is in transition.

Investment in early childhood programs

Research by Nobel Prize-winning (2000) James Heckman and his group indicates that a proactive approach to developing economic and social skills through investing in quality early childhood programs is more effective and economically efficient than trying to close the gap in the future. The view is that we profit significantly from these investments in the early years. Because programs aimed at the early years are the most productive – investing heavily in a child's skill base allows for higher returns later.

The research is based on a forty-year experimental study of a program under the supervision of Hackman and his colleagues. This method is based on teaching through active learning and participation. Active learning means students learn through direct contact with people, objects, events, and ideas. This program was conducted in a 'Perry' preschool in Michigan, USA.[28] The designers of this study provided detailed economic conditions to determine whether there is a net benefit, i.e., a positive return, from investing in early childhood education programs to facilitate social mobility. Research designers calculated social rates of return based on secondary differences between early childhood interventions, which included the long-term benefits and harms of education to public welfare. The result that the designers of this project obtained is that the economic return of increased investment in the form of early childhood educational intervention yields annual social return rates of 7% to 10%, which is about 2% more than the stock market. The figure below shows that investment during preschool gives a higher rate of return than in the time of school and post-school.

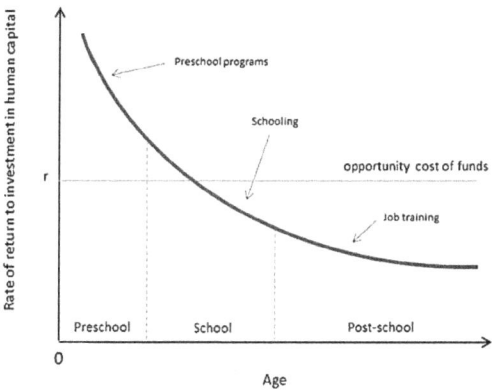

Figure: Investment during preschool gives a higher rate of return

Research has shown significant long-term health effects for disadvantaged children, including early education, nutrition, and health. More than forty years later, people in the treatment group had a significantly lower risk of developing serious diseases like stroke and diabetes. These findings show the great potential of coordinated programs from birth to five years of age to prevent chronic diseases, reduce healthcare costs, and create a prosperous society.

This research shows that the highest rates of economic return come from the earliest investments in children's education, providing insight into the future as society invests more money in later development. The highest rate of return in early childhood development is due to investing in families as early as possible, from birth to five years of age. Investing in disadvantaged families is especially important. Heckman believes that starting at age three or four is too late because it is impossible to recognise that talents create skills in a complementary and dynamic way. Efforts should be focused on the first years to be most efficient and effective. The best investment in quality growth is childhood from birth to age five. Such investment is very effective for disadvantaged children and their families.

Having established that education and training and the formation of human ability respond positively to investment in early intervention, the solution to deprivation can be redefined away from paying low-capability people not to be poor towards paying to raise capability. However, a strategy of substantial investment in the widespread implementation of early intervention schemes to facilitate social mobility is much easier to justify and promote if there is a net benefit, that is, if there is a positive return on the investment. Thus, it is essential to correctly identify the relevant costs and benefits used in calculating the return on investment in the early intervention scheme.

Education for higher economic growth

Investment is needed to create economic progress in every country and at all times. Investment is necessary in all aspects, including expenses that lead to maintenance, survival, increase of production capacity, types of equipment, and development of natural resources. It should be noted that expenses are included in more than just the material or physical area. It also includes human resource development, research and development, education, in-service training, and health and labour movement. The most essential measure that should be taken in relation to economic growth and development is to invest in human resources to increase a nation's capital. The main reason for the low level of economic growth in developing countries is the shortage of skilled people. Until the level of skills and professionalism of the workforce is not improved, the productivity and efficiency of the workforce remain at a low level. Hence, the education of people plays a vital role in a country's economic growth in creating skilled people. The people of every society have a significant role in the growth and development process. There is nothing that leads people to prosperity and perfection as much as investing in education and training.

Regarding the study of the impact and the role of education on the economic growth of developing countries, they have obtained such results that education is one of the main reasons for economic growth and development. Today, it is known that there is a significant relationship between education and income of people. More education brings higher skills to people, which are in the field of producing goods and services that stabilise the market condition and accelerate economic growth.

In terms of economic growth and development, countries are at different stages. For example, investing in children's education is crucial for economies in transition. Developing countries can achieve higher economic returns in the future. Unfortunately, many of these developing countries do not give it vital importance and have yet to understand the significance of this matter. Several other countries are waiting for international organisations to help them. And for several other governments, the priority is spending in areas that are not beneficial for the generality of the population and social welfare. Also, parents need more knowledge and information about the importance of children's education.

The World Economic Forum (2016) suggested three channels through which education affects a country's productivity. First, it increases the collective ability of the workforce to carry out existing tasks more quickly. Second, secondary and tertiary education mainly facilitate the transfer of knowledge about new information, products, and technologies others create. Finally, increasing creativity boosts a country's capacity to develop new knowledge, technologies, and increased outputs. These channels, no doubt, have been used by a number of countries, such as China and India, to be transferred with significant economic growth.

Education is a leading determinant of economic growth, employment, and earnings. Ignoring the economic dimension of education would endanger the prosperity of future generations, with widespread repercussions for poverty, social exclusion, and sustainability of social security systems. Consequently, spending on education is becoming more of a priority worldwide. Education is widely accepted as a leading instrument for promoting economic growth. For example, in several developing countries where change is essential, education of higher education is critical to solving several societal problems, such as population control, increasing employment opportunities and coming out of poverty. So far, governments have placed great emphasis on primary and secondary education. But now it is realised that higher education, particularly the enrolment of girls, is an effective solution to control and manage population density and poverty eradication. Therefore, lacking attention to higher education is crucial for economic growth.

Quality early education and development programs for disadvantaged children can foster and discover talents, create diverse skills, strengthen the workforce, generate economic growth, and reduce social costs. Investments in children's education can also lead to job gaps in the labour market. Of course, awareness and recognition of investing in children's education are more visible in developed countries. In the more advanced countries, governments have set aside a significant budget to educate children from the age of four. Of course, as discussed, it should be noted that although investment in early childhood is essential, it is not the only factor of economic development, and other factors should be considered.

Conclusion

Human capital has long been considered the most distinctive feature of every economic system. Improved education leads not only to increase individual income but is also a necessary precondition for long-term economic growth and prosperity. There are many reasons for the resulting outcomes. Education can be defined as the stock of skills, capabilities, and other productivity-enhancing, which are some of the characteristics of an economy in transition. Education is a critical component of a country's human capital that can increase each individual's efficacy and capability. It helps economies move beyond traditional and simple production processes. The history of more advanced nations has proven the crucial impact of education on improving productivity and growth. The priorities are improving the economy, strengthening the middle class, and reducing poverty and inequality. Solving these challenges starts with investing in a country's most excellent resource, its people.

Chapter 11 -
Exploring human happiness

Introduction

If you look at some of the pictures posted online, it is said that people experiencing poverty are the happiest people. Are, really, the poor people the happiest? No one can honestly answer this question or agree with this view. My experience living among people experiencing extreme poverty for two decades is that they are more content with what they have because they cannot gain access to a better life. How can a hungry, poor-health person with no home, filthy clothes, and poor hygiene be happy? Have these people chosen such a life, or do they have no other choice? A picture of children laughing is posted online, and comments say that these children and their families are happy people. But do these children know the concept of happiness, or have they tried it? So, what is happiness?

What defines happiness?

No one can tell us how happy we are except ourselves. Happiness is not genetic; it has to do mainly with individual character. Although everyone is free to define happiness in their terms, in practice, the things chiefly cited as determining happiness are, for most people, much the same, including material circumstances, good health and education, work-related factors, family and friends, community consideration, environmental consideration, consideration of other people and other places, a certain level of freedom to live as desired, and to have opportunity to progress. These are some of the universal principles for happiness.

Sometimes there is enough happiness in our life, but we cannot recognise them, or they are hidden. Hence, we have to discover them. A Spanish proverb says that happiness is like a candle that is turned off; however, it has the potential to be lighted and benefit from its light and heat. Happiness is feeling good, enjoying life and feeling it as excellent, satisfied, joyful, delightful, hopeful, and a positive energy to serve others. Unhappiness is feeling bad and wishing things were different. We can define happiness as a mental state of well-being and positive emotions. The concept of happiness is, in some ways, influenced by culture and society, the expectations society puts on a person or family. For example, with increasing materialism, feelings of inadequacy and wanting more become vital in one's perception of self-worth. For example, wanting more and more of the same thing is what makes some people very happy. This is the basis of consumerism, one of the challenges of our time. The challenge is finding a balance and standing up within oneself to the pressures that may surround us to have more things or make more money. In many ways, it comes down to what we prioritise as our highest values in life and how we may focus on them.

When discussing this subject, we can identify four groups of people with different attitudes towards happiness:

i.   Those who are never happy.
ii. Those who are happy if certain things expected of them are reached.
iii. Those who think they are not happy but will be happy in the future.
iv. Those who are happy all the time.

Genuine laughter is a good sign

People with laughter or smile are more attractive to others, they can produce positive energies, and their joy affects their family members, especially if the laughter is accompanied by kindness. In Japan, the power of smiles and laughter has been recognised, and in business, it is a part of customer service to attract more customers. For example, in some companies, staffs gather in a circle every morning before starting work and laugh loudly for about thirty seconds. Also, employees have learned different techniques for practising smiling. Therefore, smiles and laughter can be used as a tool for business competitiveness. The view is that a happy workforce is a motivated workforce. Therefore, happiness is highly valued in today's society. Not only do people aim for joy in their own life, but there is also growing support for the idea that we care for other people's happiness.

Factors determining happiness

Happiness is like short-term and long-term plans. Most of the time, it is long-term happiness that is real happiness. We must plan which type of happiness we want, short-term or long-term. Most people are looking for short-term satisfaction. For example, there are many enjoyments in life which give us short-term happiness: like laziness, sleeping, watching TV, and listening to music. All these provide short-term, temporary satisfaction, and it is here that short-term enjoyment turns into long-term unhappiness.

Happiness also should be discussed with time and space. Once upon a time living in caves and jungles was a kind of happiness, but today a certain amount of living standard is necessary. Many of us remember when the telephone was a luxury item; today, it is necessary for most people, especially concerning our occupations. In 1979, during our stay in Bangladesh, after four years, we could afford to buy a second-hand fridge. The day we purchased that fridge was a happy occasion, although the only thing we could put in it was water. The fridge was a part-time utility because, most of the time, there was no electricity at night. Therefore, happiness should be discussed with time and space.

Can money buy happiness?

There is a paradox in our society. On the one hand, people want more money and want to become more affluent. On the other hand, as people get richer, they have not become happier. Once, a very successful and famous footballer, whose monthly salary was more than a million dollars per month, said, 'I am broke'. Another successful and renowned footballer with a massive income said, 'I have a miserable life.'

On the one hand, people want more income to become more prosperous. And on the other hand, as people get richer, they have not become happier. Those with more income can better fulfil their aspirations; however, income growth does not necessarily cause happiness and well-being to rise. The correlation between happiness and income in an individual is highly significant but is very low. Of course, income is essential, but it is not the only factor affecting happiness. The happiness may be weakened by other variables such as unemployment, better training, or family circumstances. So, it is a combination of factors that makes a person happy or unhappy. Happiness depends on extra money when people's income is near the poverty line. But if people's income is above the poverty line, happiness is independent of capital and income. Hence, happiness varies during the life cycle depending on the circumstances, including infancy, childhood, young adulthood, adulthood, and old age.

Happiness creates a balance between our abilities and our expectation. While happiness may be material, it may have some aspects of higher values. Let us consider the following example. Life is like driving on a motorway. There are always some drivers ahead of us and some behind us. If we accept that all drivers must go to a particular destination and go their way, it doesn't matter if we are ahead or behind other cars. In economic terms, if we have our objective for life, it doesn't matter socially and economically; we are ahead of others or behind.

Now on this busy motorway, if at all times we want to look at others and try to speed and pass other cars or in other words, in life, if we want to look at others and see how they are doing and try to compete with them, for two reasons we will be sorry for our action. One is that we must put extra pressure on oil consumption to take over other cars. If our vehicle is not strong enough, we may damage the engine. Compared to our life, we may put too much pressure on ourselves and become depressed. In this situation, we will witness other cars passing us without paying attention. And secondly, even if our car can speed up and take over other cars, the police may stop us, and we have to pay a fine. And even if the police don't catch us, we fear the police seeing us. In real life, as we expand our business, we will be watched by the law.

Therefore, knowing our limits and measuring our speed according to our capacity and requirements is better. This requires having a good plan. In this way, individually, we will be satisfied and happy, and at the same time, we won't hinder others. This way, we all can work together for society's general progress. According to this example, happiness is considered as establishing and maintaining a balance between opportunities and expectations that leads to good mental and physical health. Therefore, happiness creates a balance between our abilities and our expectation. Also, we must work towards creating and achieving happiness, which becomes exciting. For example, reaching the top of a mountain is an achievement; however, all the excitement is when we climb up to the top.

Happiness through employment

The concern for employment in society is significant for growth and development. It can affect the lives of individuals and families to enjoy a higher standard of living and make them happy. Young people should not be excluded from this practice. The younger generation, in particular, constitute the active segment of the society. Hence, guiding them towards the right work path can contribute to the development of their living conditions and the whole of society. Knowing that many countries face various economic problems, young people can create significant changes for their country by working in the right field and making themselves happy. Young people are valuable resources for the country but lose their golden years for work due to various obstacles. Knowing these obstacles and finding suitable solutions for them seems the right way to create job opportunities for young people.

True happiness

Considering the duality of human nature, an adequate description of true happiness can be described. Humans possess a spiritual or higher nature and a material or lower nature. The virtue of benevolence belongs to the higher nature of human beings and is a source of true happiness. In other words, true happiness is associated with higher nature, and material or physical happiness is related to the lower nature of human beings. Therefore, true happiness for rich people is sharing their wealth willingly, becoming more sensitive, and showing compassion towards others. Perhaps one reason the rich countries help the poorer nations is that they have realised that in an integrated global society, the problems of the poor will become the problem of the rich. People will be happier if the material aspects of their lives are fulfilled and developed alongside kindness and compassion towards those experiencing poverty. In other words, the material and spiritual coherence principle advocates that there must be a balance between the two parts of life.

Conclusion

There is no doubt that many of the joys of life cannot be compensated with any amount of money, such as spending happy moments with family and close friends or putting smiles on the faces of children that we can try to improve their lives. Sometimes, it is necessary to look at the course of life and our goals and consciously take steps in the path of life. Each person defines happiness differently with specific values and tries to reach those standards, and after some time, assess whether by reaching those factors, we got the satisfaction of joy we expected or not, and if necessary, our outlook on life should change the course of our activities rather than imitating people whose goals in life are different from ours.

Contrary to a completely materialistic view of life, if we have an altruistic view, providing material facilities with more money for ourselves may not have any effect on the feeling of happiness because an altruistic and generous person cannot enjoy his luxurious lifestyle when he sees several needy people and working children who are making a living in an inappropriate situation. For a person who sees his well-being as a part of total well-being, helping someone in need or serving people will bring more happiness than having more money. Therefore, with such a view, money is a means to meet needs and help the community's total well-being. It is such a joy when money buys happiness for the community.

Chapter 12 -
Is broken capitalism fixable?

Historical questions

Are the capitalist system and the free-market economy governed according to the theory of liberal classics, have the character of self-repair, self-regulation, and self-correction? Is government intervention in economic processes necessary or not? These historical questions have been on the agenda of political economy theorists in different ways since the birth of capitalism until today.

Economists from the time of the industrial revolution in the 18th century until almost the middle of the 19th century, such as Adam Smith, David Ricardo, and John Stewart Mill, have dealt with these questions. They believed that in a capitalist economy or an economy based on a free market, the invisible hand of the market could solve its problems. Fluctuations in supply and demand, overproduction, and unemployment in periods of recession and prosperity are inherent in capitalism. But the market mechanism solves the problem of falling prices and increasing unemployment over time. They said government intervention would create more problems. The economy should be left to do its job. Without denouncing these views, in 1936, John Maynard Keynes supported active government participation, specifically at the macroeconomic level.

Can today's condition of the economy be improved after more than two centuries of a capitalistic, free-market economy? Our focus in this chapter will be on the three inherent pillars of this system, namely, the minimum or absence of government intervention in the activities of the market, the view on self-interest, and the issue of competition. The aim is to suggest that economics in transition requires government intervention, collective interest rather than self-interest and cooperation instead of competition.

Capitalism versus free-market economy

Knowing the difference between capitalism and a free-market economy would be helpful. In theory, capitalism focuses on creating wealth, capital ownership and production factors, mainly land, labour and capital. A free-market economy focuses more on exchanging wealth or distributing goods and services. Its operation is through an invisible hand working with techniques of the price system and competition.

Therefore, the capitalist in a free-market economy works independently and with maximum freedom without government involvement. However, the free-market economy allows minimum government intervention in the exchange part. The role of government is more of a watchdog; they intervene when required, which is different from central planning, known as a planned economy or command economy, with total government involvement in all aspects of the market and the economic life of citizens.

The processes by which capitalism emerged, evolved, and spread worldwide are the subject of extensive debate among historians. The history of capitalism is diverse and has many debated roots, and it has mainly emerged in Great Britain and the Netherlands from the 16th-17th century. Of course, a variety of capitalism started many centuries back from the time which was known as Laissez-fair capitalism with no government intervention (laissez-faire is a French term that translates as 'leave alone'), then to industrial capitalism or free-market economy capitalism with little government intervention, then to welfare capitalism with much more government intervention for reasons such as the implementation of laws and government-funded social programs, and to more modern forms of the corporation and financial capitalism with extensive market regulation. Therefore, as we see, the role of government has changed from almost non-involvement to active interference in all aspects of the market. The degree of involvement in the economic life of people varies from country to country. For example, there is maximum government involvement in a country like North Korea and minimum government involvement in the United States of America. In the middle, we may name Great Britain and India.

The Dutch model focused on moving goods from markets where they were cheap to where they were expensive. The focus was on trade rather than on production. Therefore, the building-up of wealth by merchants was without the emergence of capitalist production. However, the Great Britain model created wealth through industrialisation and production methods, especially during the industrial revolution and the need for capital accumulation associated with the concentration of wealth and economic power. Therefore, during this time, free-market capitalism gradually became the dominant economic system in Europe and slowly spread worldwide.

The mid-18th century gave rise to industrial capitalism, which was made possible by three reasons:

(1) the accumulation of vast amounts of capital to be invested in machinery. (2) the fact that Britain had a large population who needed to buy essential commodities through the market, which required a mass consumer market. (3) Britain could export its manufacturing products to the rest of Europe. As we see, capitalists performed the job of capital investment, and the free-market economy exchanged capital and distributed products.

This system of free-market capitalism has several advantages, including efficient allocation of resources, cost reduction, efficient production, less wastage of resources, and a democratic decision-making system. These were necessary for increasing the profit as a means needed for financial incentives. However, free-market capitalism is inherently exploitative and unsustainable and creates economic inequality. In the 20th century, capitalism changed its face from investing back capital for manufacturing purposes and the possibility of benefiting the economy to a type of capitalism with uncontrolled, unregulated, unlimited and unrestricted challenges, including greed, self-interest, selfishness, relentless competition, excessive power, control and wastage of the Earth's precious resources, corruption, exploitation, misleading promotional activities, and in recent time encouraging consumerism and materialism as a lifestyle. The focus here will be based on three fundamental principles inherently rooted in the system: relentless competition, self-interest, and the minimum or absence of government participation. Most capitalists are aware of the challenges of free-market capitalism, and the time has come to either fix it or end it.

Government involvement

Adam Smith founded free-market capitalism in 1776 and discussed it in his book, The Wealth of Nations. This book is considered the essential guide to be followed by capitalists for wealth creation during and after the industrial revolution. One of the principal features of the free-market economy of capitalism is that the government should have minimum involvement in economic activities. The market should be free to decide what is suitable for the participants. The view is that actors of the market are rational thinkers, and a market reaches equilibrium or balances itself automatically. The instrument of invisible hands, which includes price system and competition, influences all market participants to make the right choices. Hence, there is no need for government to intervene.

Today many economists express the notion that a crisis, such as external shocks that may happen at any time, will expose some of the flaws of this kind of thinking and that the market has failed to save the lives of people and a failing economy. We experienced two such shocks recently: the 2008 global financial crisis and the 2019 COVID. Both examples required active government intervention.

Suppose the main motive of a capitalist is profit maximisation, but numerous activities in society do not generate profit. Consequently, active government intervention is needed urgently during an external shock. Most of the time, there is no profit for the private sector to participate and handle such a colossal task; government intervention was vital. For example, with COVID-19, on the one hand, governments must step in and inject a financial stimulus package into the economy. On the other hand, try to slow down the spread of the virus to protect vulnerable populations. In a free-market economy based on profit intensive, these activities are not those in which a free-market economy is interested.

The challenge, however, was that this Pandemic happened suddenly, and governments needed to prepare and be equipped to deal effectively with this crisis because the expectation was that the market would take care of it. The current Pandemic is only one example; other instances of market failure include the absence of necessary and sufficient resources, shortage of human resources expertise, short-termism, politicising decision-making, etc. The result has made public-sector institutions ineffective when we need them to overcome crises. The government needed to be adequately prepared and equipped to deal with such a crisis in such economies.

Here are a few suggestions for the government to become more effective:

- Governments must invest in and create various institutions to deal with crises.
- Governments need to coordinate research and development activities better.
- Governments need to structure public-private partnerships to ensure effective and efficient use of resources so that everyone benefits economically.

Therefore, government intervention in the market becomes necessary to balance the economy and advance a more equitable society, which also benefits the market. Government involvement is required in areas where the free-market economy is not interested because little or no profit is available. Hence, a government with the right plans and adequate resources can control and regulate the economy.

Self-interest

Another fundamental principle inherent in the free-market economy of capitalism is self-interest. The view is that we are naturally endowed with a powerful desire for bettering our condition, which, according to Adam Smith, "comes with us from the womb, and never leaves us till we go into the grave."[29] His famous example of butchering tells us, "It is not from the benevolence of the butcher, the brewer, or the baker, that we expect our dinner but from their regard to their self-interest."[30] Also, he said, "...every individual ... naturally prefers himself to all mankind."[31] These powerful statements support the self-interest of the founder of the free-market economy of capitalism.

Of course, Smith does not denounce social justice and benevolent activities. Still, the emphasis is that benevolent activities are outside the market, and self-interest is for the market to function correctly. In other words, the phrase economic man is for the inside of the market, and spiritual man is for the outside of the market. If we accept and agree that the market is a part of the whole society, then the market is included when the entire society is prosperous. In other words, the market becomes a means to create a prosperous society.

To expound on this topic, it would be helpful to distinguish between self-interest and selfishness or self-love. Self-interest is when a person is concerned with his well-being and engages in activities that benefit him and fulfil his desires, which could also affect others positively. However, a selfish person with characteristics of self-love is excessively and exclusively concerned with himself, purely seeking his wishes and desires without regard for others. In self-interest, a choice must be made, which is the best choice for a person. Most people make most of their choices in their self-interest. We need to denounce selfishness and self-interest for a meaningful and enlightened global society that includes the world's citizens. The view is that humans make choices that promote common interest rather than self-interest. These choices would lead to effective and efficient use of resources and the distribution of goods and services equitably among members of society.

In balancing self-interest versus the common interest, one's self-interest is also included in the common good. If one makes efforts so that one's community is prosperous, it will also ensure one's prosperity. With all the horrifying experiences we had with the current Pandemic, things have happened that are signs of the truly altruistic nature of human beings, and this is demonstrated by all sorts of people and business organisations as a part of transforming available resources for the benefit of a community, small or large, without knowing who the beneficiaries are.

The view of true happiness discussed earlier; is associated with the higher nature of human beings. Consequently, self-interest and self-love belong to the lower nature of human beings. At this level of living, there is a need for understanding the proper place of material pursuits in one's individual and family life, in carrying out meaningful living conditions, transforming self-interest into collective interest, and in a quest for true happiness and prosperity.

Competition

Let us recall the need for competition as one of the pillars of the capitalistic, free-market economy during the industrial revolution with an increasing level of manufacturing products. Competition was necessary to motivate capitalists to invest more and create a competitive market to sell innovative products. Heavy investment by the capitalists, on the one hand, and division of labour, on the other hand, was the cause of increasing output. Manufacturers needed a much bigger market than the United Kingdom to distribute their products. There was a need to attract the rest of Europe and, beyond that. Competition played a significant role in the process of distribution and efficiency purpose. For example, through competition, businesses use resources more efficiently, resulting in less waste and less cost. Also, with competition, companies produce better quality goods and services to attract more customers. In theory, consumers benefit from both lower prices and better quality. Therefore, the fact that consumers, to some extent, can benefit from the competition cannot be overlooked.

However, competition has changed its face. In practice, through aggressive and relentless competition and an uncontrolled market, small and vulnerable businesses are destroyed and eventually exit the market. Others are scared to enter the market because they cannot compete with those giant corporations. This behaviour in the market leads to the creation of uncontrolled and unregulated monopolies. The result would be higher prices, lower quality, waste of resources, fewer choices for consumers, and market control. More seriously, if one of these large corporations fails in a global market condition, the entire economy could suffer. Therefore, relentless competition is one of the world's leading causes of economic injustice today. One remedy is to observe moderation in all aspects of life. The business model is another aspect of life and must function in moderation. Why should some corporations become gigantic, and when they fail or become bankrupt, causing society to suffer? The principles of moderation and market regulation will ensure that the market functions more justly for all the participants.

Relentless and aggressive competition without government regulation may lead to greater corporate domination in the market, which, in turn, may lead to the removal of smaller firms, causing numerous challenges, including a higher unemployment rate. For example, how can small family businesses operate and survive when large multinational companies with the advantage of lower costs operate in developing countries? Or how can family businesses with no information technology and capital investment survive while big corporations are equipped with the most advanced operational techniques? To maintain high profits, these transnational companies move to any part of the world that can access workers with lower wages and easy access to natural resources and lower tax rates. Such actions destroy small firms and family businesses, which are an essential source of employment. Hence, small and family-based companies will face enormous challenges in a heavily competitive market.

In modern times, organisations use social and ethical responsibility as a 'unique selling point' for competition. The moral principle of moderation also applies to the expansion of trade. The excessive growth of work and the scale of business may become a visible problem for a market, to the environment and, in several ways, a disadvantage to an organisation itself. The consequences of unlimited expansion can be detrimental and unsustainable, with numerous damaging effects, both internal and external. Sustainability requires a kind of economic growth without environmental damage. Moderation dictates a limit to an unlimited expansion. Of course, the character of some types of change can be limitless and indeed is commendable, such as growth and development of the arts, training and education, service to humanity, philanthropic activities and acquiring morality.

COVID-19 was a reason to convince the urgent need for cooperation rather than aggressive and relentless competition. Today, the interdependence of the peoples and nations of the world is a fact. The analogy of the human body can be used to express that interrelationship of nations and peoples exists from every aspect: socially, politically, economically, environmentally, and morally. Pain and suffering in one part of the human body is the cause of discomfort in the rest of the body. Similarly, pain and suffering in one part of the world is the cause of pain in other parts of the world. The current Pandemic is a clear example of the interconnectedness of people and nations; hence, the crucial role of cooperation must be considered and appreciated. Applying the principle of cooperation would allow smaller businesses to enter or stay in the market without the fear of competition forcing them out. It, therefore, stimulates enterprise, thereby helping employment, increasing the output level and generating more revenue for the government. This is the message of the people of the world frequently repeated during COVID-19; it is stated in chapter one and worth repeating once again: 'At this moment, we feel more united wherever we live than ever before, even at a distance.'

Conclusion

The current free-market economy with a capitalist foundation is difficult to be fixed in the short run because its fundamental principles of self-interest and relentless competition are rooted in the system. However, in the long run, the system should not be defeated but fixed for the benefit of the entire society. A sensible, equitable and sustainable economic system in transition needs a free-market economy that is adaptable to local conditions with universal values. With this view, government intervention will be required but at a minimum level and focus on activities that the market cannot perform.

Chapter 13 -
Significance of the middle class

Introduction

To guarantee a just distribution of resources among the citizens of a country is to strengthen the middle class of the economy. The middle class is a social class and includes many people in different jobs who are more similar to the upper class in terms of cultural values and more identical to the working class in terms of income. One of the characteristics of economics in the transition is the existence of a middle class with a high percentage.

One of the characteristics of most societies is its class characteristic, which can be classified into three categories from an economic point of view:

    i.   The wealthy, the high-income, the consumer-oriented, and the prosperous class.

    ii.   The poor or low-income, the deprived, and the working class.

    iii.   Between these two classes exists the middle class.

Regarding the fair distribution of wealth in the country, it is necessary to create jobs for all citizens, especially youth. In this case, governments should use three principles: economic freedom, equal opportunities for all, and the existence of the necessary means for progress. Of course, today's economy is very complex and requires economists to constantly manage economic resources, including human, financial, physical, and natural resources. It is necessary to use these resources optimally. Effective management in both private and public sectors makes people try to participate in economic activities more effectively. For example, even though taxes are high in some countries, people pay taxes happily because they know the government has a reasonable budget. For people to pay taxes happily, the government must act responsibly and spend money sensibly and accurately by practising justice and fairness for the period they are in charge.

The crucial role of the middle class

Why is the economic middle class reduced or even destroyed in some countries? To answer this question, several issues are of concern:

- In terms of employment, this class mainly works in clerical and service work or factories. In the last few decades, large multinational organisations have entered the labour market and are engaged in mass production, which is sold at a low price. These products have also entered developing countries, threatening many businesses, including the middle class. This has also caused a decrease in income. Decreased income means the middle class must settle for a simpler life, which is characteristic of deprived or underprivileged people.

• The deprived class is used to the hardships of life, and economic crises affect their lives less. But for the middle class, economic problems such as unemployment and inflation cause a big blow to their lives, and this group should make significant changes in their lifestyle and enter the deprived class.

• Most citizens of Western European countries are considered middle class. How did it happen? In 2010, the percentage of people in the middle class in Spain, Denmark, the Netherlands, Norway, France, England, and Ireland increased from 60% to 80%. Therefore, these countries are prosperous and deprived classes are decreasing.

• Bangladesh has made significant progress in increasing the number of the middle class in the last 40 years. In 1975, the wealthy class constituted 5% of the population. Today it is more than 10%. In 1975, the poor part of the population was 90%. Today it is 50%. In 1975, the middle class in the country was 5%. Today it is 40%. As we see, a significant part of the 'have-nots' classes has moved to the middle class by reducing the number of 'haves' classes. How did this happen? A few examples are mentioned here:

- Compulsory education at primary and high school level for girls
- Encouraging girls to do higher education.
- The role of international trade by providing more employment opportunities to the 'have-nots' class.
- Women empowerment and improving the family living condition.
- Reducing corruption in both the private and public sectors.
- The Role of Grameen Bank in Micro-Credit Finance.
- Reducing religious, ethnic, and economic discrimination.
- In the 1980s, Bangladesh's biggest challenge was the high population growth rate. Today, it is under control because of the heavy investment in education, especially for girls from primary to university levels.

As we see, a significant part of the 'have-nots' classes has moved to the middle class by reducing the number of 'haves' classes.

This is the middle class, which on the one hand, wants to reduce economic corruption in the upper class and wants to eliminate it. And on the other hand, they are heartbroken for the deprived people in society and want a better system to establish justice. The middle class aspires to enjoy knowledge, insight, freedom, and democracy in the community. This group has noticed the progress of other countries and feels its lack in their own country. The middle class realises that the economic problems are increasing, and they think about the deprivation of society or the poor class. The existence of the middle class is fundamental for a country's economic growth and development.

Also, the middle class is witnessing economic corruption in the private and public sectors and is trying to correct the situation. In most revolutions based on crime and corruption, the middle class had two things in mind: bread and housing for the deprived and freedom and democracy for all. Therefore, the middle class of society played an important role and caused the revolution's victory. The deprived and the upper class have played a weak position, and the middle class has played a prominent role in improving the system.

Now, if this middle class has such power, it should try to protect itself and think of the disadvantaged in society, and this is where the economic role of the middle class becomes prominent. What should be done is to transfer the deprived class to the middle class. Western European countries, Canada and Australia and several others have done the same and are somewhat successful. Of course, governments have a significant role to play, which means the transfer of the poor class to the middle class and, at the same time, the wealthy class to the middle class. Therefore, the middle class has received the attention of governments in every way .

One of today's economic problems is the increasing gap between the haves and have-nots. Of course, the condition of 'have-nots' has not worsened in most areas, but the state of 'haves' has become wealthier faster. In most countries, the middle class's economic life is improving, but not enough. Of course, every person and family prefer to move to the upper floor, but how? Unfortunately, the societal situation is such that the distance between the affluent and deprived classes is increasing.

Now the question is, if society's successful and underprivileged classes are destroyed, will there be rich and poor in the middle class? It depends on how we define the middle class. What is essential is that the incomes will be different. People's income depends on many factors, including education level, skills, talent, motivation to work, and working conditions. It is essential that everyone has the minimum economic and social rights and includes features such as food, clothing, housing, education, health, economic freedoms, opportunities, and means necessary for progress and work motivation. In this middle class, there will be people with different incomes. What is essential is that all citizens are given economic freedom, equal opportunity and means to develop. Any classification that creates a gap between people regarding human rights is unacceptable.

Conclusion

To conclude this chapter, let's raise this question: if society's well-off and worse-off classes are reduced or eliminated, will there be rich and poor in the middle class? It depends on how we define the middle class. What is essential is that the incomes will be different. People's income depends on many factors, including education level, skills, talent, motivation to work, and working conditions. It is essential that everyone has the minimum economic and social rights and includes features such as food, clothing, housing, education, health, economic freedoms, opportunities, and means necessary for progress and work motivation. In this middle class, there will be people with different incomes. What is essential is that all citizens are given economic freedom, equal opportunity and means to develop. Any classification that creates a gap between people regarding human rights is unacceptable.

Chapter 14 -
Consumerism: A great challenge of our time

Introduction

Consumerism is one of the economic phenomena that gained a significant boom after the industrial revolution, particularly in the 20th century. Considering that human life depends on the planet's available resources and the limited access to these resources, correcting the consumption pattern is particularly important. It is special, especially with the advancement of knowledge and information technology, the expansion of urban life, the mass production of industrial products, the increase in the scope of advertising activities of various media, and the encouragement of more consumption of consumer goods, we are witnessing the unrestrained trend in consumption by the present generation. In order to find the goods produced usefully and as a result of buying and consuming them, humans have left a very devastating effect on the mental balance of people in different societies. As a result, they create alienation and various obsessions in large groups of people. This consumption pattern is wasteful. It is rooted in some human societies' excessive and uncontrolled freedom and greed. Consumerism is the cause of the destruction of the ecosystem, which causes the reduction and destruction of the resources needed for the life of all the planet's inhabitants. It is cruel to the present and the future generations. It requires a suitable strategy for the proper management of resources and a change in the lifestyle of the citizens of the whole world.

In modern times, goods and services have moved out of their traditional form and are no longer to satisfy a group of natural needs; instead, their consumption is symbols and signs of status and personality. Consumption is a tool to show the social status considered by the consumer. Consumption has been introduced as a means of creating identity, and consumers try to develop and preserve their identity by consuming and displaying commodities in their possession. The culture of the new world has considered consumption as a criterion and character property as a means of identification, which has led to an increase in consumption and the emergence of a kind of consumption competition among people in society.

The logic of consumerism is that increasing demand for goods and services leads to economic growth and makes everyone enjoy a better economic life. The logic for businesses is that: consumption needs more production, more production requires more workers, and the more workers are in the labour market, the greater the economic activity. This itself causes rapid economic growth. Therefore, more consumption is beneficial for everyone. The logic from a consumer perspective (not all) is that more of the same thing and of everything makes a person happier and more satisfied. The view, in theory, is that individuals who consume goods and services in large quantities will be better off. But does this type of reasoning make sense, or it causes severe challenges that lead to consumerism?

For this discussion, a number of definitions are helpful: Consumption is related to purchasing goods and services necessary for life, making life difficult without paying attention (economic view). Consumerism is one of the general characteristics of modern society in acquiring more and more unnecessary goods, and it is mainly considered among the luxuries of life. (This is an issue related to a combination of disciplines, including economic, social, and spiritual). Materialism is more related to the attachment of humans to material things, one of the characteristics of individuals in a society (philosophical view).

We hear the phrase 'enough is enough' in our day-to-day conversation. The phase of 'enough is enough' or 'far beyond actual necessities' is the stage in which one is already satisfied, and no more will be tolerated. Spending 'beyond actual necessities' or the stage of 'enough is enough' means buying more unnecessary products and possibly diminishing our happiness. Beyond the set of 'enough is enough', overconsumption has led to a consumer society, causing the wastage of resources. The 'beyond actual necessities' stage corresponds with 'the law of diminishing return', which states that our satisfaction diminishes as we consume more of something. Hence, if we are happy and satisfied with a certain amount of something, why should we have more of it? Stopping beyond necessities means we are healthier and, at the same time, saving resources for more deprived ones. So, what is the rationale for consuming more than enough?

The root idea flowing from self-interest is consumer sovereignty and utility maximisation. The rationale is that consumers know their interests best and can act to advance them through the exchange. The difficulty is when the market fails to function correctly, and consumers fail due to the need for the necessary information to make the right decision.

Consumer sovereignty and utility maximisation become more sensible and sustainable once the market functions appropriately and achieves an 'equilibrium of interests' and consumers have the necessary knowledge and information about the market.

Causes of consumerism

There are several causes for doing consumerism.

Human desires are unlimited: When this phenomenon is combined with greed, the cravings will be incomplete. Therefore, buying goods out of greed is one of the important causes of consumerism.

The role of advertisements: The most important factor causing consumerism in the acceptance of advertisements among the general public is the cultural values hidden in them. The role of advertisements is such that after a short period and after the release of a new product, by presenting new models, it causes the rapid decline of the previous product and the replacement of the new product that is more attractive. The new product is more attractive, complete and better. Nowadays, countries' economic income depends on their commercial advertisements.

Human wants can be limited if the income is fixed: But since income is increasing in most societies and most markets, especially in more developed countries, the demands of most people are either rising or cannot be controlled.

Wants are often complementary to each other: This means a group of goods completed together, such as several foods and household items. The type of completion of goods together depends on the income of individuals and families and relies on the lifestyle of people. And whether individuals and families are used to a life of luxury or not.

Human wants usually compete with each other: For example, we have a TV, and a better one enters the market, and we buy it. That means we compete with ourselves in our own homes and with our home items. When we realise that the house is full of things that have been bought, several pieces of each type, this is also a form of consumerism.

Habits: Human wants become habits, even when people's income is fixed or when faced with unemployment. In these situations, many people are burdened with debt because unwilling to give up habit.

The discount seekers: Many customers look for the best deals they can find. These customers are interested in buying a product when they see a reduced price tag on it. It is not a matter of the necessity of a product but related to a reduced price. Undoubtedly, commercial advertisements with the aim of introducing goods and services are one of the necessities of the present age. Sadly, this type of advertising, using some images and some beautiful words and content, has caused the spread of consumerism in society. Commercial messages, while distancing themselves from their primary function, which is the introduction of goods and services, have created a sense of need in the audience, thus fuelling the increase in consumerism that provides the interests of capitalists. In commercial advertisements, something that is not important at all is the need for essentials and more attention and importance to consumption. The important thing is that there is no need to pay for more consumption, but getting a product for free is the reason for happiness. For example, buy one and get one free. Or buy now and pay after two years. Therefore, people are encouraged and motivated to achieve happiness through consumption. Most ads emphasise the word discount, which in a way bewitches a person to buy it without thinking and paying attention to the product's actual value and regardless of their need, just because the product has a discount. For a child who grows up in this environment, getting discounts and free items becomes a goal in life. One, who grows up in this culture, is used to consumerism and blindly looks for advertisements, does not consider their needs, and only consumes. One who gets the goods with the most significant discount is more successful, and this cultural value is collected. The capitalist system will only be able to survive with consumerism. Therefore, searching for consumption markets in other countries is on the agenda. Therefore, part of the duties of the family, education and the government are to teach the correct consumption at different social levels.

A few additional points for causing consumerism:

Low-income group versus high-income group: with the poor and low-income group, all or a large part of their daily or monthly income is usually spent on the necessities of life, and there is nothing left for savings. With the wealthy and high-income group, the needs of life are more or less fixed, of course, considering that the conditions are of high quality. This is an unnecessary part that leads to consumerism, such as similar goods, goods that are constantly changing, buying similar things, or their attractiveness. Millions have come from absolute poverty in the last few decades and have higher incomes. The argument is that this group also has the right to enjoy a modern and better quality of life.

Therefore, some characteristics of consumerism can also be seen in this group.

Role of monetary policies: Another cause of consumerism is the monetary policies of the government or the central bank. To reduce unemployment, for example, the government reduces bank interest rates. In this case, people prefer to spend their money rather than save. And since the essential part is more or less fixed, more expenses are made in the non-essential part. The challenge is that the high demand for non-essential goods causes wages to rise nationally, including the wages or salaries of workers who produce essential goods. An increase in wages leads to a rise in prices; therefore, this monetary policy of the government or the central bank causes those with low incomes to have trouble buying essential goods.

Role of credit cards: Another cause of consumerism is the credit conditions of consumers, which are done through credit cards. If they are not used properly or misused, these credit cards will be one of the worst tools that make many people go into debt because they spend quickly, but they can hardly pay the debt on time, usually with much interest payment. Of course, the system of many markets and banks is set so that the validity of these credit cards is higher than banknotes.

The need for sufficient information: Individuals and families often need correct and adequate information about the goods and services available in the market. At the same time, due to the need for proper knowledge and awareness, they may be deprived of buying some essential products. In both cases, the market will witness a shortage or surplus of some products. This action also leads to market imbalances.

The challenges

A review of the terms 'needs' and 'wants' will be helpful for this discussion. Traditionally, a lack of resources is considered a fundamental problem. When resources are scarce, consumers are forced to make choices. In the eyes of consumers, these choices are based on what they consume. Needs are essential and fundamental and must always be met. However, it is only sometimes possible to satisfy all demands because when one is satisfied, another demand arises. This point is especially true in the markets of innovative products. Therefore, although it is possible to meet human needs, it may only satisfy some human desires due to limited resources and unlimited wants.

Economists call this phenomenon of endless demands the term 'ostentatious extravagance'. This term refers to people who want to live above the subsistence level, which refers to the 'affluent class'.

This question should also be raised, is consumption the highest goal of an economic system? Here, the purpose of life for humans in the consumption of goods and services should be examined. Suppose the meaning of life consists of values such as serving humanity and being aware of the needs of others; then, the whole perspective changes. With such an attitude, everyone takes care of each other and tries to serve others. With this point of view and having a purposeful life, environmentalist expert Arthur Dahl believes that goods and services that harm the environment, do not have the characteristics of sustainability and reasonable consumption and are not in line with human dignity will disappear from the market. For example, most weapons production, industries that support ostentatious extravagance and luxury goods, most misleading advertisements and cruel competitions, and products such as pornography, and hard drugs, were removed from the market. Harmful industries may be money producers and guaranteed business that considers human material life, but they will not bring people peace of mind and conscience.

But what alternative is suggested for the economic losses caused by eliminating those goods and services that are unnecessary or harmful to the environment? This argument makes it possible that in a dynamic society, without unnecessary commodities, there are opportunities to produce alternative goods and services that are more valuable, useful and befitting for human dignity, such as more social services, educational opportunities, increasing the possibility of research, and much more. Also, there will be development and innovation in various fields such as education, healthcare, food and agriculture.

Also, suitable work opportunities will be created for more than one billion unemployed people living in poverty. These numbers from the low-income group join the middle-income group, which makes work and positive activities. Human society is constantly growing and developing. Therefore, science, industry, technology, and human innovations will reach that stage of evolution that will produce and supply all kinds of jobs suitable for humans, especially for half of the world's population who do not have access to an ideal life. Therefore, the durability and sustainability of life with reasonable consumption is an effort to take good care of the earth's resources. Its purpose is to meet the needs of this generation while supporting resources for future generations and preserving and respecting the environment. In the long run, a moral balance and economic stability will develop.

Consumer education

Several principles can inspire people to make appropriate decisions about purchasing goods and services. They can give people the knowledge to consider the advantages and disadvantages of goods and services or distinguish between genuine and misleading advertisements. Knowledge, information, and ethical values are critical determinants of market efficiency. Therefore, the quality of information directly affects the ability of the market to meet society's collective material needs.

The consumer determines the success and failure of every business organisation. Consumers are the reason for continued product production, hence sustaining a business. The success of every marketing plan must begin with the consumer and depends on whether the marketing plan has considered consumer behaviour. Such consideration is necessary for the marketing plan to succeed. Similarly, the success of all aspects of a product, including its price, quality, shape, colour, size, taste, and distribution channel, depends on the satisfaction of consumers. Ultimately, consumers can influence producers, manufacturers, suppliers, and intermediaries to deliver goods and services according to consumer choice.

Therefore, 'consumer sovereignty' is an expression that signifies the power of consumers to determine what goods and services need to be available in the market. In other words, consumers can primarily determine how resources are allocated. Keeping in mind that the effective allocation of resources is one of the fundamental principles of economics, consumer education helps to allocate resources more effectively and efficiently. Under this condition, consumers become more responsible and vigilant towards resources and people's needs. Such an education is necessary because of the vulnerability factor of specific consumers, such as income, age, education and health.

Consumer education is also helpful when dealing with the issue of consumer capability, for example, freedom from limitation and rational decision-making. It also helps with comparability and the complexity of information that comes with various marketing techniques. As the market becomes more competitive, there is also the issue of differentiating between products, which requires a certain level of knowledge and information to enable consumers to distinguish between them. The authorities in the UK have taken several steps to assist 'consumer education' and thus influence sustainable consumption.

What is stated so far is that consumer behaviour can directly benefit consumers in a more formal sense. The acquired knowledge can serve as data and information for developing educational programs to improve consumers' decision-making regarding products and services. Consumers will demand non-exploitative products as they become better informed about a sustainable lifestyle. Consequently, successful organisations would be those that respond positively to demands. Consumer education is vital in improving decision-making in an age of materialistic attitudes and market complexity. One advantage of the ability approach is that it recognises individual as well as social variation in the level of consumption needed to achieve a sustainable lifestyle.

Despite the effectiveness of consumer education and the way it can influence firms to produce goods and services that are sensitive and sustainable, producers have the power to influence consumers through marketing techniques. The remedy consists of legislation regulating the market, which can run alongside consumer education. In practice, consumer protection laws are established in most countries under the banner of 'consumer rights.' Regarding ethical consideration, we can define rights as natural rights, which are those essential, necessary, undeniable, and befitting entitlements that should be respected and protected at all times.

The concept of rights was introduced and led to the United Nations Charter of Human Rights, issued in 1948. This has been a powerful standard for the worldwide enforcement of various fundamental rights. The most recent manifestation of this is the Charter of Fundamental Human Rights for the European Union, which was agreed upon in the Nice Treaty in 2000. In the United Kingdom, Consumer Protection Law, under the supervision of the Competition Commission and the Office of Fair Trade, also protects consumers.

Consumer education must achieve sustainability. The issue is not about what product or how much of what product, but the question of why a product? Hence, the focus would be on why a product is needed rather than what is required. Increasing consumer and producer knowledge and responsibility greatly influence why a product is necessary.

In many instances, the need for sufficient consumer knowledge and information leads to the under-consumption of merit goods and the over-consumption of demerit goods. By definition, merit goods with positive externality are those goods and services that are valuable to an individual and beneficial to society, such as education and vaccination. In other words, the benefits to society exceed the private benefits. Demerit goods with negative externalities, such as using hard drugs and gambling, are unsafe to individuals and society. Similarly, there will be under-production and over-production, leading to shortages and surpluses of output. The consumers' actions and producers' reactions lead to a waste of resources, both human and physical. In this way, consumer education can significantly influence the market to allocate resources effectively or, in economic terms, achieve equilibrium. If well informed, consumers can shape the social impact of corporations, and even their size, through their expenditure decisions. Moral leadership is also needed in addition to consumer education for a sustainable mode of production. On a practical level, sustainability requires maintenance and social responsibility at both the individual and corporation levels. Thus, consumer education, corporate social responsibility and sustainability go hand in hand.

Balancing our lives

In a free-market and from the perspective of the founders of classical economics, equilibrium occurs when buyers and sellers intersect at a point in the supply and demand curve. At this point, buyers and sellers agree on the price and quantity set in the market. In other words, at the point of equilibrium or the intersection of supply and demand, the actors in a free-market think rationally. The problem with this type of equilibrium is that at the point of balance, some goods and services are offered on the market that are harmful to human health and destructive to the environment. Also, certain levels of regulation are needed to ensure that the products produced are sustainable and not damaging the planet's valuable resources. The view here is that at the equilibrium point, the free-market actors should think rationally and act morally so that the market moves sensibly during the transition towards a sustainable economy.

Moderation should be considered an effective solution to the problem of consumerism and balancing our lives. People should reach a stage of maturity to define moderation for themselves because it has different concepts and meanings for others. The stage of maturity can be seen as when a person has reached the point intellectually, morally, and spiritually to be able to take responsibility for himself and others so that the wealth acquired can be spent sensibly and responsibly. This also can be interpreted differently because a person's maturity level affects the spending of wealth on products suited for human dignity. This way, producers are inspired to produce sustainable products, and the market is responsible for selling ethical products to meet consumers' demands.

Conclusion

Consumption, no doubt, is crucial and sensible for the functioning of the economy. But not consumerism. Consumerism is an economic and social issue that encourages the acquisition of goods and services in ever-increasing amounts. In some cases, the reason for this increase can be external factors such as advertising and economic policies; it can also be internal factors such as the belief that buying more will bring more happiness and cause a better living. Consumerism can also cause damage to the environment because for the production of many goods, much pollution is produced, and valuable resources of the planet, such as water, are used in large quantities, which its shortage can harm the environment. The most critical factor in the growth of consumerism is the media and attractive advertisements, which can control people in many decisions. People can reduce this problem to a great extent by using optimal decisions and rational and moral choices and causing less damage to people, animals and the environment.

We should reduce and even eliminate the expenses that are destructive and harmful to the human world, the planet, and the future generation, reaching a balance in the socio-economic body. Balance in socio-economic life is still related to social and economic stability, which includes the minimum welfare for all citizens of a society, including eliminating extravagances in society. Therefore, conditions must be created to guarantee relative well-being for society.

Chapter 15 -
Moderation

Introduction

Materialistic ideologies, including unregulated capitalism and ego-centred values, underpin the economic problems of over-consumption and, as a result, consumerism discussed in the previous chapter. For an effective action to tackle the problem of consumerism and related extreme materialism, economic theories such as the theory of demand in microeconomics (classical), aggregate demand in macroeconomics (new-classical), and utilitarian theory,[32] which is money-orientated, would not be appropriate. These theories need to be revised to deal with the challenges of consumerism and establish sensible, equitable and sustainable consumption as a requirement for a healthy economy. Moderation in all aspects of life is one way of balancing the economy without depriving ourselves of the manifold benefits of the available products.

Definitions

Moderation is an economic sustainability that requires balancing the lowest and highest living standards. One extreme is when the rich enjoy the greatest extravagance and comfort, and the other extreme is when the poor are in absolute poverty. Therefore, moderation is a condition when there will not be the abnormally rich or the abject poor. The rich and poor will enjoy the privilege of an improved economic situation. Henceforth, this model's economic description of moderation is expressed as eliminating extremes of wealth and poverty.

For a topic such as consumerism, we must distinguish between consumerism and living well. Sustainability is associated with living well but requires living in moderation. There is a correlation between moderation and sensible and sustainable living. Sustainable living is a lifestyle in which one enjoys resources with consideration for other people, the environment and the future generation.

Moderation is a situation of balancing, controlling, limiting, and restricting our actions towards a sensible lifestyle. In our day-to-day living, moderation in food is seen as simple, enjoyable, healthy, sustainable, lawful, and thoughtful. It is also described as moderate in various senses regarding conduct, opinions, demands, and desires or their indulgence. Moderation avoids extremes, especially in behaviour. Moderation at the societal level is the elimination of extremes of wealth and poverty. But any future economic system should be able to prevent wealth accumulation in a few hands.

Moderation, if practised sensibly, can balance all aspects of individuals' material life and solve the societal problems associated with extremes. One may wonder if we spend and consume sensibly because of the economic conditions or because by doing so, we acquire virtues. We may be spending sensibly and practising moderation due to economic conditions; nevertheless, we accept and try to acquire virtues by exercising this principle. The moral implication is that one should be kind and compassionate, share with those in need, and have empathy and understanding for those with inadequate living. It also requires protecting the environment and respecting the future generation. Moderation necessitates control of one's selfish desires and refraining from greed and self-indulgence. If we define the purpose of economics as an art of effective and efficient use of resources, then moderation and greed would be at the opposite poles. Desire leads to the wastage of resources, while economics aims to reduce and prevent wastage. All of these are virtuous qualities that, when applied to others, will help us grow physically, mentally and spiritually.

Moderation also has important implications in economics through resource allocation. The exercise of moderation is commendable in all things, including in trade. The lack of control over the growth and the enlargement of organisations may lead to the creation of monopolies. The out-of-proportion expansion can be challenging for the economy and disadvantage the organisations. One of the difficulties of such out-of-proportion development is the creation of monopoly power and its undesirable and harmful consequences, including wastage or lack of appropriate control over resources, problems of coordination and cooperation among various departments, and a barrier to desirable competition. Why should some of these organisations grow so much that the whole economy suffers if they fail or go bankrupt and exit the market? Since large companies hold a significant market share, the entire market would face a crisis if they fail. Thus, a moderate expansion of trade is safer for organisations and the whole market.

The view is that moderation requires a limit to economic growth. However, economically certain specific industries must remain large, known as 'natural monopolies'[33]; otherwise, they will suffer from 'diseconomies of scale'[34] that are not beneficial to consumers and the wider society, such as water, gas and electricity companies. A desirable competition is healthy for the whole economy as well. By desirable competition, I mean morally suitable activities that serve the advancement of wider society.

The extent to which moderation is necessary for the progress of a country varies from one economy to another. In the initial stage, for example, an economy requires faster and higher economic growth to achieve reasonable take-off. Expert in economic growth and development, Walt Rostow, in 1960 considered five stages for economic growth, namely: 1) traditional society, 2) preconditions to take-off, 3. Take-off, 4. Drive to maturity and 5) age of high mass consumption.[35] The take-off stage is crucial to economic growth. This stage requires substantial human, physical, and capital resources, plus adequate savings and investment. Hence, the moderation exercise may be less helpful at this stage, particularly for less developed countries. Indian and Chines claim that it is their right and opportunity to have high economic growth. The argument is that once upon a time, the existing developed countries got the chance to have high economic growth, leading to enjoying a high standard of living.

Going back to Walt Rostow's view about the stage of growth, he needs to explain what happens after the age of high mass consumption. Is mass consumption the ultimate goal of human life? Economically, one can consider the term 'extravagance' as the production and consumption of unsustainable products that bring about the wastage of rare earth resources, environmental degradation, and consumerism. The take-off stage is associated with flying, but the flight cannot be kept hanging in the sky; it must eventually land. There is no explanation if mass consumption is the primary purpose of life. Hence, moderation, recommended in all aspects of life, must be a part of the theory of Rostow, even during a period of abundance.

The exercise of moderation varies among people and depends mainly on individual and family circumstances such as the size of the family, employment, the level of earnings, and the pattern of individual and family lifestyle. For example, what kind of moderation is suggested for those in absolute poverty? Moderation for those living in absolute poverty requires moving to a higher standard of living. Not only government should have appropriate plans for uplifting the standards of life of the lower income group, but people have to show responsibility to move up to have a better lifestyle.

We should also distinguish between a moderate way of life, simple living, and asceticism. Voluntary simplicity or simple living can be described as when individuals or families, by their own choice, reduce the consumption of goods and services to their basic needs or avoid the accumulation of wealth. Voluntary simplicity is different from a situation where individuals are poor and are forced to spend less or have a simple life because, for example, they are unemployed. Simplicity, however, may not be constructive for economic reasons. For example, it may cause unemployment, slow economic growth, and less government revenue and its consequences on public services. However, voluntary simplicity adopted as an alternative lifestyle differs significantly from the simplicity forced on people with features of poverty. Lower consumption or simplicity may lead to high unemployment in the short run. However, in the long run, the world is full of purposeful, productive and satisfying jobs waiting to be done in areas such as education, urban renewal, environmental restoration, childcare, and health care. A simple needs-orientated economy with moderation will better address urgent concerns.

People may choose simple living for different personal reasons, such as health, increased quality time with family and friends, stress reduction, personal taste, a reaction to materialism, and support of an anti-consumerist movement. Simple living is not living in seclusion or practising asceticism. Asceticism will not help an economy and a sustainable lifestyle. Most human beings, to some degree, experience physical suffering throughout their lives; however, it should not be invited or made into a way of life.

Conclusion

Eliminating the extreme gap between the rich and the poor cannot be done overnight. This will be a gradual process. An example would be that when people use all the good things in abundance equitably and sensibly, there will be no need to produce unnecessary, damaging, and destructive products. This way, resources will be saved for improving the lives of people experiencing poverty. The legitimate privilege to derive the absolute advantage and benefit from this world's manifold joys, beauties, and pleasures requires a high standard of moral conduct. Maintaining such a high standard of behaviour in all aspects of life, it is left to the discretion of individuals to decide their degree of moderation, as this may vary from person to person.

Chapter 16 -
Making sensible and ethical choices

Introduction

In the words of Aristotle: "Excellence is never an accident. It is always the result of high intention, sincere effort, and intelligent execution; it represents the wise choice of many alternatives – choice, not chance, determines your destiny."[36]

Basic concepts

Let us begin with this question: Shouldn't morality also be a part of human behaviour to make sensible choices? In other words, when making a choice, do I primarily consider what is best for me, or do I think what is best for me and the people around me, or do I believe what is best for others that will also positively impact me? This simple question lies at the heart of significant differences between cultures and individuals. Of course, most people are not very selfish as to ignore all others or so selfless as to ignore their own needs and wants entirely. Apart from these two extremes, cultures can still differ when discussing the subject of choice.

In academia, various views on how to deal with economic issues exist. But there is an agreed level of understanding about the fundamental economic problem in one area. The economic crisis means that because of scarcity or limited resources and our unlimited wants, choices must be made by consumers, businesses, governments, each individual and family unit. As we cannot have everything we want, we must arrange our list in order and give preferences to those at the top, indicating that we must give up or sacrifice some of the less important ones. In other words, there is an opportunity cost. Opportunity is what we gain; the cost is what we must give up or sacrifice.

Alternatively, it would be advantageous to examine the working of the market and to know how it functions under different conditions and see more clearly what is valuable and what is not. For example, markets give consumers a choice of commodities to buy, which is helpful. However, the selection of items on the market does not necessarily reflect what people want to buy or what is good for society. A part of the market mechanism is a device adapted to serve the community's goals. Hence, resources such as land, labour, and capital are justified only if they benefit the community. Also, resource holders such as entrepreneurs must act in ways that benefit the community. Since production is going to be repeated, acceptable choices by consumers become essential for purchasing commodities in the market. Other issues concern false advertisements, which mislead innocent and more vulnerable customers into purchasing items they would otherwise not buy.

Rational Choice Theory

Economists have been using the idea that people make choices in rational ways and that all we need is to put the collected information into mathematical formulas for a chosen and satisfactory result. Many factors may drive any choice behaviour. Combining various social sciences can produce an intellectual collaboration that leads to a better description of our world.

The approach in economics is to collect quantitative data and fit it into a mathematical formula. Still, this procedure is inappropriate in the real world, with millions living in the same society and having different behaviour towards life. This seems less than an adequate representation of the real world. In real life, we come across many things that our common sense tells us different things rather than measurable mathematical formulas. Once their impact is thoroughly explored, we will only know whether social sciences, such as psychological or sociological factors, are relevant to economics. We are in a perfect time to conduct such a study. For example, we are at an ideal time to explore people's behaviour towards self-interest, utility maximisation, consumerism, and relentless competition. Mathematical formulas are not able to tell us such behaviours. Also, a purely mathematical dimension of economics cannot explain why people are still living in absolute poverty with so much advancement in economic life and increasing the wealth of nations.

Of course, the importance of mathematics cannot be ignored. The vast contribution of mathematics in many areas of research is evident. Applying mathematics in decision-making is essential for making difficult choices in public policy, health, business and finance, banking, manufacturing, and many other activities. Mathematics evaluates and improves the quality of information, and economics is about improving the quality of life. Therefore, having the correct data is crucial. It should, however, be realised that having the right information is only one aspect of making choices. The basic idea of rational choice theory is that collective social behaviour results from the behaviour of individual actors, each of whom makes their own decisions. The role of the individual is a critical factor in making decisions about choices that are both rational and sensible.

Personal choice based on self-interest

The school of classical economics advocates that the individual's happiness is important and that the success and growth of an economy are based on self-interest. Rational choice theory is an economic principle that states that individuals always make sensible and logical decisions. Given the choices available, these decisions provide people with the most significant benefit or satisfaction and are also in their highest self-interest. Most conventional assumptions and theories are based on rational choice theory. Early economists writing about sensible choice, including Adam Smith, argued that if each person pursued his economic self-interest, society as a whole would benefit, stating that: "every man is, no doubt, by nature, first and principally recommended to his care ... it is not from the benevolence of the butcher, the brewer, or the baker, that we expect our dinner, but from their regard to their interest."[37] Also, Adam Smith, in *The Theory of Moral Sentiments*, states, "every individual...naturally prefer himself to all mankind."[38] John Stuart Mil (1844) wrote, "The only freedom deserving the name is that of pursuing our good in our ways."[39] William Stanley Jevons

(1871) assumed that people make choices to maximise their own happiness or maximise utility. These statements tell us that in a capitalist society or free-market economy, selection is based on individualism, which is taught to focus primarily on self-interest and happiness.

Self-interest is when a person is concerned with his well-being and engages in activities that benefit him and fulfil his desires, which could also affect others positively. According to economist Michael Parkin "In self-interest, a choice has to be made, and that choice is the best one available for a person. Most people make most of their choices in their self-interest."[40] A view would be making choices that promote common or social interest rather than self-interest. These choices would lead to effective and efficient use of resources and the distribution of goods and services equitably among members of society.

When we look at Karl Marx's model of collectivism is based on a minimum standard of living for all citizens. However, talking about choice, during the communist period in the USSR, the government provided everything; the government made all the choices for the people. People couldn't make any choices and had little control over their own life, but a minimum standard of living was provided for all citizens. In a more capitalist society, people are free to make all kinds of choices, have freedom, and control their own life, but the difficulty is that many people have no money to buy what they choose.

Researchers have done several experiments on infants and animals, concluding that choice is a natural phenomenon. The need to control our own life is genuine. People can manage their lives and choose from different options in free societies. In communities without freedom, people are not in control of their life. One of the reasons for the failure of the Communist regime in the USSR was that they tried to take away freedom from people. People wanted to make their own choices, and not others chose for them. Today, a similar thing is happening, for example, for women. In many cultures, women can't choose the type of life they like; men decide their life patterns.

Why make sensible choices?

The critical issue is that there are alternatives. Choice means that one option is selected over another. In the absence of alternatives, there is no need to make choices. In a more advanced society, people have to make many choices because of high expectations, and people are dissatisfied when they lose the attractiveness of alternatives. Therefore, to be satisfied, people buy more similar products to enjoy the attractiveness of alternatives. This has led to consumerism, one of the challenges of our time.

Nowadays, there are so many choices we can make for the same kind of product. Once upon a time, there was one type of car in America, and it was easier to choose because there was only one kind. Though one car is perfect, our expectations went up. People now expect to choose improved products, and producers must develop better products daily to satisfy our expectations. In an affluent society like America, the expectation has gone up, and some people cannot meet all their expectations and, as a result, are less happy. Even in a country like India, once upon a time, a 'simple life' was the norm; now, the slogan of 'India Shining' has created consumerism for a minority population and left behind millions of farmers and others in the villages with no opportunity of a better life. The poor people in many places are not given the opportunity to develop their capabilities and talents, and those in authority are not showing interest in discovering those talents. In order to make sensible choices, prerequisites are necessary, such as providing economic freedom, opportunities and the means.

Choice and decision-making

Although the words choice and decision-making are used interchangeably, the two have some differences. Choice leads to decision-making. In other words, decision-making is based on preference choice. Choice refers to the act of accepting a selection. Therefore, the choice is there when there are alternatives; if there are no alternatives, there can't be any choices.

Decision-making, however, is a process to reach the end of a selection procedure. A decision results from a thought process that begins with choices or opportunities. Therefore, a decision implies the selection of one of the choices. For example, in a question paper, students are given three or four choices of possible answers that they must choose from and tick their preference for the correct answer. The decision indicates that we have finally concluded. Here, choice represents various possibilities, while decision reflects the final choice. Our choices are often influenced by our belief system, culture, family circumstances, personal habits, income, work, and what others offer us.

Equal opportunity, equal rights, basic needs

Choice and equal opportunity: Choice and equal opportunity is based on the thinking of political philosopher John Rawls (1921 – 2002). According to him, all individuals should have the same opportunity to choose and create a life and a livelihood that will allow them to acquire the things they value.

Equality is an opportunity to ensure that access to material and social resources is justly distributed. In other words, it creates opportunity and the importance of providing means to accompany options.

We should also note that everyone's talents and abilities are different; therefore, their economic contribution to society would be additional, but the opportunity should be there for all. According to John Rawls, ambitious people who want to work hard to acquire wealth should be able to do so. People who choose not to take as much advantage of these opportunities can accept a lesser economic condition.

Choice and equal rights: Choice and equal rights are based on the thinking of economist Amartya Sen - the Noble Prize Laureate in 1998. On equal rights, societies often specify certain rights to which each individual should have a similar claim, such as liberty or the pursuit of happiness. According to Sen, a rights-based interpretation of equality is that equal rights are more fundamental to well-being than a particular level of material goods. There has yet to be a universal agreement on what these rights should include or how they should be related to economic issues. Among the things suggested by some countries as everyone's rights are free education and free health care.

Amartya Sen maintains that poverty based on income deficiencies does not accurately show how poor a population can be. He has suggested that one's capabilities should be considered — that is, the choices and opportunities people have to be well-nourished and have access to education and improved health condition are more important than a simple income measure. He emphasises the goal of enlarging people's choices, which depends fundamentally on equal rights and building capabilities. According to this principle, the success of a society should be judged not by its members' average or total well-being but, instead, by its treatment of those who are worst off.

John Rawls has proposed a general approach to the question of the worst off. When discussing the choice with justice, he suggests two criteria: First, each person is to have an equal right to the most basic liberties. Second, social and economic inequalities must be arranged so that the most significant benefit goes to the least advantaged. Here, the first principle ensures that essential freedom should be realised before proceeding to the next step. Based on this view, if the poor are listed under the category of the worst off, then support should be given to the idea that in social and economic activities, the most significant benefits should go to the least advantaged. Also, the first principle ensures that essential freedom should be realised before proceeding to the next step. The remedy must be legislative for the application of such views.

Optimisation of preferences

Economic theories begin by making assumptions about people's choices and preferences and the question of what those preferences are. In most cases, people try to 'rationalise' their choices that are compatible with the optimisation of preferences. For example, regarding food and preference maximisation, in distributive justice, the first choice should be given to those who need it more, which means the preference should be given to poor people.

What definition should an economist use? There is no simple answer; different people have firmly held political and ethical preferences for one or another concept. For some, how much inequality is tolerable or desirable and what policies are appropriate to achieve this desirable level? What definition is closer to ethical economics? On the one hand, the paradigm is changing from the individual to that of the community. On the other hand, individuals associate choice with freedom and the existence of equal opportunity and the provision of basic needs for all.

Let us imagine we are in a society where freedom and opportunity exist, and other principles and values, such as becoming a productive member of the community, and service to others, become a part of the culture of a society. This way, we maximise the welfare of the community while having the choice for our own life. Our identity becomes a matter of choice. Once we choose our individuality or originality, the selection process becomes more accessible. We make better choices once we know why we are created and the purpose of life. So, the choice model would be ethically acceptable and economically ideal when it benefits the individual and the greater society.

Are fewer choices better in economics?

Can we argue that poor people are relatively happier because they are more content, have fewer expectations, and fewer alternatives are available to them to make choices? From my experience living among people experiencing poverty, there is a difference between living simply because people chose to do so and living merely because they have no other choice. In other words, the wealthy person can decide on many options. At the same time, a person experiencing poverty does not live that way.

Alternatives become challenging when we allow others to make choices for us rather than make our own choices according to our values, such as contentment and moderation in all aspects of life. When we know that the standard for selection is ethical principles such as justice, why we are created, and the purpose of life, there are no hard choices to make in economic life. Once children grow up with values, knowing the meaning and purpose of life, and a culture based on virtues is established, it becomes easy to make ethical choices. Because we are social beings, our identity is shaped by and shapes our society.

Conscious and sensible choices

Several guiding principles can influence producers, consumers, and other actors in the market to make conscious choices about what to produce and consume. The following principles will be helpful:

- The principle of universal and compulsory education assists in making a distinction between merit goods and demerit goods.

- The focus of agreement between science and morality helps one become conscious of the benefits a product offers consumers and its effects on the ecosystem.

- The consciousness and realisation of the principle of unity make it possible to adopt a more sustainable lifestyle and save resources for the benefit of those in need, and a personal commitment and a more comprehensive loyalty to the whole of humanity. Such an attitude will effectively influence sustainable living.

- The theme of service is central to the understanding of sustainable consumption. Service to humanity is closely associated with the ethical concept of compassion and caring. Compassionate people have a deep awareness of the suffering of others.

- The consultation model helps individuals collectively to make well-informed choices and hence make a final decision to live a well-balanced life.

Reflection upon these guiding principles can elevate the consciousness of individuals to a higher level and help them become more considerate in using the valuable resources available to them and, at the same time, use monetary means more sensibly.

A particular version of the choice theory involves looking for the most cost-effective means to achieve a specific goal. The economic idea of the input-output model can be used to explain the rational choice theory. It is the process of converting inputs to produce output. In this model, the choice is a process that, in economic terms, requires a cost-benefit analysis. We can choose to use all the resources available to make those destructive, harmful, and unnecessary products for humans and nature, or we can choose to use resources to produce necessary, ecological, and beneficial effects. Once human talent, capability, knowledge, wisdom, and moral and spiritual consideration are added to transferring input into the output, producing output becomes useful, valuable, and ecologically sound. Therefore, ethics should be considered another resource for conscious choices and added to the input section.

In self-interest, a choice must be made that would be the best option for the person. Ethical decision-making would make choices that promote social interest rather than self-interest, which is the best for the wider society. In this case, making choices leads to effective and efficient use of resources. It distributes goods and services fairly, equitably, sensibly, and sustainably among members of society. Therefore, it is argued that education will help consumers make sensible, wise and conscious choices. To achieve sustainable consumption, there is a need to influence supply and demand. On the one hand, consumer education and acquiring and applying value principles, on the other, will enable a successful process. Hence, willingness to change lifestyle and to control and modify excessive consumption is suggested.

Economist James Buchanan, known for his 'Public Choice Theory, in his paper entitled 'Fairness, Hope, and Justice, argues that economic justice is derived from a sense of fairness. To influence this fairness, he focuses on distributing rights and claims before the market process rather than on some final product distribution. Buchanan is aware of consumers being handicapped due to their vulnerability and self-interest. Thus, he proposes intervention by the government before the market process. For example, he advocates taxation for public financing of compulsory education. It is the level of consumer education that would affect making conscious choices. Consumer behaviour needs to be channelled either through moral acts or through legislation.

Conclusion

There is no quick guide or set formula to make a conscious and sensible choice; it is a process that requires individual talent, capability, knowledge, and ethical qualities to make a final decision. The option is giving preferences to our needs and wants. People must choose which desires to satisfy and which they will leave unsatisfied. In an economic condition where resources are limited and wants are unlimited, choosing is a critical approach to distributing resources more fairly, justly and efficiently. Consumer behaviour should either be controlled by laws or by ethical principles. To impact the choice, emphasis should be given to creating a culture of moderation. The moral implication of choice is that each household consumes the goods and services needed for a healthy lifestyle and a sustainable economic climate.

The choice theory should not be criticised based on the preference of utility maximisation and self-interest but need to be corrected and modified in how individuals can make the right choices that are socially desirable, economically preferable, environmentally suitable and morally acceptable, in a sense that our choices are guided by virtues that are helping the well-being of individuals and the common goods.

Chapter 17 -
The model of economic freedom, equal opportunity, and the means

Introduction

The model introduces elements necessary for the economic development of individuals, families, and the whole society. These elements are prerequisites for making the economy more equitable and sustainable.

Economic freedom

Freedom refers to releasing ourselves from all forms of prejudices. There is significant economic development by removing various prejudices leading to discrimination. Freedom is the ultimate goal of economic life and the most efficient means of realising general welfare. Amartya Sen attempts to redefine economic development, not in terms of Gross Domestic Product, mainly based on monetary values but on the fundamental freedoms people enjoy. According to him, there is higher economic growth in countries with relative freedom in all strata of society. Also, countries that practice gender equality and religious freedom are more creative and economically advanced. Sen addresses the question, what is the connection between our economic wealth and our ability to live as we would like? Based on this view, if a government restrict freedom, it hinders the economic development of a whole community. Without appropriate freedom, citizens cannot demonstrate their full economic capability and cannot live a life of their own choice. Everyone should have the right to a comfortable life. The phase of 'comfort' is the stage of self-support and sustainability or a condition of genuine happiness. This is where individuals and families can choose a safe state of well-being.

Economic freedom is a phenomenon people experience in a given society in pursuit of their interests. Hence, the ability of individuals in a community to take economic action is more in the interest of individuals in society as a whole about productive activities. The ideals of economic freedom are strongly associated with healthier communities, cleaner environments, greater per capita wealth, human development, democracy and poverty alleviation. Financial freedom is a term used in economic and political debates and the philosophy of economics. Economic freedom is one of the hallmarks of an economic system that it may or may not have. Capitalist systems, for example, typically experience greater economic freedom than communist or socialist systems. This freedom can be exercised through free-market with low levels of government participation, free trade and adequate protection of private property. On the other hand, economic freedom can be guaranteed by having a diverse market in which consumers have many options to meet a particular need. Also, the job market should be free to allow individuals to pursue a job based on their talents and desires, rather than limiting the scope of their options to government policies or any other restrictions.

Equal opportunity

Freedom to choose is necessary for creating relative comfort, but more is needed. All citizens must have equal opportunities to benefit from their talents and capability. How can there be freedom without equal opportunity? In the same way, how can there be a free-market economy when there is no equal opportunity for all the participants? The operative spiritual principle for a more regulated free-market is exercising moderation at all market levels. True freedom must be found within the confines of what is seemly moderation so that humanity has a future for generations to come. Therefore, lacking moral and ethical consciousness on the part of businesses, or the inability to stop or do less of a bad thing without a stick from an authority, makes the world worse off, with less equality and thus more injustice.

When discussing distributive justice, the perspective is that absolute equality is neither possible nor practical nor justified. Equity is preferred to quality. This view indicates that individual talents and abilities are different, and hence their economic contribution to society varies; however, the justness of opportunity should be there for all. In economic discipline, economic justice is about equity rather than equality. The earnings of each person depend on one's productive contribution to society. However, it can be argued that the goal of social justice is for people to be equal. The view is that we are all equal, not because we are the same but because we are all equal in the sight of the laws of the land. This suggests that each person has certain rights granted by a constitution. These rights include the right to life, liberty, and the pursuit of happiness. In other words, each person is unique, but human beings are not the same.

The means

How can there be freedom and equal opportunity without providing means to achieve the main objectives? For example, education is the most excellent means for the economic development of individuals, families, and communities. The history of developed nations shows that they have achieved success by providing education to all their citizens.

Access to free and universal education is one of the most important means of development and is considered one of the rights of the citizens of a country. It is a basic human right, and the Universal Declaration of Human Rights emphasizes this right and pays special attention to it. Clause 1 of Article 26 of the declaration says: "Everyone has the right to education. Education shall be free, at least in the elementary and fundamental stages. Elementary education shall be compulsory. Technical and professional education shall be made generally available, and higher education shall be equally accessible to all on the basis of merit." Education as an important human capital that builds the conditions for creating a superior society has been emphasized in all the basic laws, and people worldwide have the right to free education. Although the level of education may vary different, it is mandatory and free because the building and development of culture and economy, as well as the intellectual development of society, is in the hands of the children and youth of that country.

A practical example of the model

The above three essential principles are necessary to implement economic justice effectively. Liberty is a fundamental human right, equal opportunity for all citizens, and the provision of means needed for development. Countries with these basic principles enjoy higher economic growth and improved living standards for all citizens. In a free society where equal opportunity is present, men and women from all strata of society can have maximum participation. The provision of necessary means enables skill learning. Skills provision requires appropriate education, training, technological advancement, and innovation investment. Opportunities are essential for the working population to apply their talents and capability. To coordinate the process of upholding the pillars of economic justice and the employment of economic resources more efficiently, the role of both private and public sectors becomes crucial in providing short-term and long-term plans.

The application of the model: In the 1970s and 80s, Bangladesh was one of the poorest countries in the world. This country has now dealt with some economic challenges, and poverty has declined to some extent. Thanks to international trade, the Grameen Bank, the government's role in reducing corruption, and the increased enrolment of girls in all levels of education. Hence, this country is currently achieving a high economic growth rate. However, in the 1970s and 1980s, Bangladesh faced a food shortage, and rice was one of the people's primary food sources. High population, low land, and lack of access to advanced knowledge and modern technology were the additional reasons for people experiencing poverty. During this time, the Dutch engineers reached them and taught them advanced expertise and modern technology. One of the ways they taught Bangladeshi farmers was that by using advanced knowledge and technology, they could harvest rice three times a year from their limited land instead of once. This made the people of Bangladesh self-sufficient in rice production, and one of the country's food problems was solved. Hence providing opportunity and the means to farmers in this country was a reason to solve the problem of rice shortage, one of the primary food sources for people.

The views of Amartya Sen

Humans have always tried hard to give an objective meaning to freedom and development, making them understandable and enabling individuals and institutions to conceive and plan in this direction. No phenomenon can be considered as the expression of these two concepts instead of humans because the human has two dimensions, individual and social, which are intertwined, and one cannot be considered without the other. Amartya Sen[41] relates these two dimensions well in his thoughts and opinions. His ideas are fundamental because they think the growth of individual freedom effectively improves the social situation, especially development. Development generally means improving living conditions, meeting needs and moving towards the ideals of human civilisation. Regarding developmental age, it is the time to achieve the possibilities hidden in freedom.

Therefore, Sen is one of the thinkers of our time who does not focus only on the economic aspects of development but considers it a multidimensional matter. The human development that Sen talks about is something beyond meeting basic human needs. This type of development respects the equality of people in achieving growth and pays attention to the empowerment of people, especially in the matter of choice. In general, it can be said that Sen's opinions regarding development and freedom are concentrated and meaningful under the banner of empowerment.

We should not ignore that every human being has the skill to develop their different abilities in the personal and social fields, so the conditions for achieving such growth should be available for every person, regardless of gender, age, race or place of residence.

An active and dynamic human being must have the ability and opportunity to shape their desired life according to the current situation and available options. Of course, some problems and crises are inevitable in social life. They cannot be prevented from happening, nor can one choose to gain wealth and social prestige by being idle and not beneficial to the surrounding society. A dynamic person with age in his mind strives and works for their life to be advanced, but this is impossible alone. Institutions in society such as the government, education institutions and business organisations should be part of shaping the development. To reach the conditions Sen is discussing, the current state of many societies, even the most advanced and free ones, will have to change.

One of the most remarkable ideas of Sen appears in his thoughts about poverty. He considers poverty to be not only the unavailability of resources and facilities to meet basic needs or low income but also the deprivation of basic capabilities. It is a human who is the decision-maker, who must define a goal, and who can achieve it by gaining freedom, ability and capability. Therefore, he spread a new view of freedom and changed it from the individualistic freedom common in Western societies to freedom, meaning the right to choose and access different choices to create a life. From his point of view, development is not a situation in which only people's basic needs are met but a situation in which people can choose from the available options and shape their desired lives with individual freedoms. In the meantime, he talks about empowerment, and in this regard, he considers poverty not a lack of access to resources to meet access needs but a lack of empowerment.

Conclusion

We are all created equal in the eyes of God, and we must be equal before the law of the land. However, we are different in ability, talent, education, motivation and the place we live; therefore, economic life will be different for everyone. However, there should be freedom, opportunities, and the means to discover latent talents and productive capacity to earn a living. It is the duty of those in charge of the organisation of society to provide each person with the opportunity to acquire the necessary talents in a profession and the means to use such talent to earn a living. Looking at the countries in which these characteristics are seen, they have higher economic growth and development.

Chapter 18 -
Combating corruption

Concepts and definitions

One of the societal ills that hinder the economic transition to a more sensible and equitable economy is the issue of corruption and its variations. Corruption exists in individuals, institutions, and a system but cannot be recognized. In corruption, contrary to other crimes, both parties are immediately involved. Hence, defining corruption is very difficult and requires a multidimensional perception from different perspectives. According to Black's Law Dictionary, the definition of corruption states: "Corruption is the offering, giving, receiving or soliciting of any item of value to influence the actions of an official or other person in the discharge of a public or legal duty."[42] Corruption creates a culture where public officials are not held accountable for their actions. In corrupt systems, laws written on paper are not guaranteed to be implemented. Therefore, what is in question is not the law, but getting to know people and how much money is to be paid becomes important. That is, relationships take the place of rules.

One of the most known to us is economic corruption. Economic corruption has always existed and will stay until government laws are thoughtfully implemented, or people reach the level of morality that does not commit corruption. The most well-known type of economic corruption that we know and is very common is 'bribery'. Bribery covers and is seen at all levels of society. Even people who do not deal with corruption are bribed, and economic damage is caused to them indirectly. Therefore, economic corruption affects the whole of society. Unfortunately, bribery is so widespread that it is one of the highest bad costs in the world, and some jobs can only be done by paying a bribe. Corruption of any kind is an economic, social, and political illness.

The most important cause of corruption is the lack of moral virtues. In other words, it is related to deviant and abnormal behaviour. For example, it is found in people who abuse their public power for personal gain. Furthermore, bribery is illegal and occurs mainly in societies where the government fails to implement laws or has weak governance.

There is a difference between bribery and gratuity or tipping. Gratuity is when someone serves you and you give a tip. But bribery is an illegal act in that a person with public influence and power does what is his duty in exchange for the amount he/she receives. This is a bribe.

Jean-Pierre Mean has explained three different types of corruption, namely: Petty and grand and judiciary corruption.

Petty corruption is the demand for a relatively small payment made by public officials. To issue a permit, ignore a violation of the law, clear goods through customs or people through immigration, obtain telephone lines, have access to education or obtain a degree. The impact of petty corruption should be considered. The poorest of the poor are excluded entirely or partly by it from many public services, including, for example, medical care, because they cannot pay the necessary bribe. Petty corruption is the ugly face of corruption that poisons many daily lives.

Grant corruption involves large payments paid to high-ranking public officials or politicians as a lump sum as a commission to obtain, i.e., retain a specific business, such as arms sales, the building of infrastructures, or a concession to exploit natural resources. Contrary to petty corruption, grand corruption remains hidden. It is often engineered by middlemen who are experts in channelling payments through offshore financial centres.

Corruption of the judiciary takes a middle place between Petty and Grand corruption. It is petty corruption in its appearance because it impacts the daily life of civil society. However, it often involves amounts which bring it closer to grant corruption. Corruption of the judiciary is particularly perverse because it deprives the honest individual of the only protection it has against the abuse of private or public power. Without the judiciary, there is no remedy against human rights violations or contractual engagements.[43]

Social and economic costs of corruption

In societies where corruption is less, it adds to social capital. Social capital means that there is a strong bond between people. They trust each other and work together more confidently. Of course, it needs to be clarified whether high social capital leads to less corruption or less corruption leads to higher social capital.

When policymakers adopt immoral and irresponsible policies and regulations, this means legislators adopt policies unsuitable for politics and economics in corrupt systems. It benefits the few with close ties to decision-makers or those who bribe government officials to pass legislation in their favour.

Such an action creates a class system in society, and the consequence is increasing the gap between the wealthy and those in the lower-income group.

One of the most important economic principles is the optimal use of natural resources. Economists condemn the destruction of the planet's rare precious resources; such destruction is immoral. Bribery is one of the concerns that cause the waste of economic resources, including human, natural and physical resources.

One of the plagues of a sensible, equitable, and sustainable economy is the formation of a class of rich people who, by increasing their wealth and power and creating informal circles, influence the decision-making process of the rulers and officials of the society for their own benefit. This problem, which is raised as an unhealthy phenomenon that exists in all societies, is one of the dangers of wealth. This hazard comes from the fact that wealth is in the hands of certain people, and financial circulation occurs between them. Bribery causes a part of natural resources to be in the hands of a small group of people, depriving the other group of use for everyday life. In other words, bribery makes a group enjoy more prosperity.

Corruption, including bribery, causes mismanagement of the factors of production (land, labour, capital). This will affect families. As a result, there will be shortages of certain goods and services in the market, which will cause the prices to increase. When the prices rise, the group attached to bribery gets the goods at a higher price quickly, which can be afforded. The price increase causes families with weaker purchasing power to suffer from a poor livelihood. Also, corruption reduces the income of the poor class of society because it destroys job opportunities in the private sector, and by limiting the service costs of the public sector, such as access to health services and education, it develops inequality. Therefore, in several ways, families with less opportunity and weaker purchasing power suffer greatly due to various forms of corruption.

Another factor related to bribery is that it reduces the quality of goods and services. This is because people who want to make more profit in the market reduce the quality of products to increase the profit.

Corruption reduces competition and efficiency in the market. When government officials demand bribes to grant licenses and certificates, it limits the number of companies that can participate in the market, resulting in profits that are not beneficial to society, and this causes companies that are unwilling to pay bribes or they don't have the power to pay it, exit the market. This means the market will suffer from less competition, creating more dominant firms with more power to control the market. This action leads to producing of low-quality products to harm the efficiency and the amount of production. In anyway consumers will suffer either by paying higher prices or being satisfied will low-quality products.

Tax evasion, which seriously threatens government revenues, is common in countries where corruption is prevalent. This happens because informal or unofficial companies do not report their profits and thus do not pay taxes. When tax evasion is common, official companies also give bribes instead of paying taxes. It should be noted that tax collection is one of the main sources of revenue for a government. Tax evasion means the government needs more funds to provide essential needs and services such as schools and hospitals, road construction and maintenance, and paying the salary of civil employees. With less revenue, the government will experience a budget deficit which means increasing borrowing.

Corruption causes a lower economic growth rate. Corruption hurts smaller companies because it is much more difficult for them to bear the high cost of corruption, including time and money, than for larger companies. In general, smaller companies have less power to avoid corruption and operate in a completely competitive environment. Consequently, they cannot recover their costs from the consumer. Therefore, where corruption is rampant, the struggle for survival is difficult for small firms and hence harms economic development since small firms act as the engine of growth. As small businesses exit the market, unemployment increases, and this causes other macroeconomic objectives to be affected negatively.

An economy full of corruption cannot correctly use the four economic principles of production, distribution, consumption, and the flow of money. Also, an economy with corruption cannot use resources appropriately, including human, natural, and physical resources. In other words, these principles of economics and resources cannot be used effectively and efficiently.

In an economy in which there is corruption, resources are not distributed fairly among the citizens of a country because part of these resources is in the hands of a few. Therefore, fewer resources will be available to others, and this causes an economic gap between people. At the government level, the income obtained through taxes is placed in the hands of the few instead of creating economic activities. Accumulation of money in the hands of a few is not healthy for an economy. At all times, money should be in circulation and become a productive resource for economic development.

Organisations dealing with corruption fear that their competitors will expose them and cause them to be arrested. In this case, productivity is lower because workers lose the confidence and motivation to work. Employees do not like or are reluctant to work for business organisations that do corrupt work. Therefore, productivity and economic progress are higher in organisations and societies with less corruption.

Combating corruption

Today, it is unanimously agreed that corruption has caused irreparable damage, and not taking action to eliminate it is irresponsible. Under the pressure of the global civil society, which consists of non-governmental, non-profit and independent organizations, governments and international institutions have made agreements to fight corruption and other commitments to improve governance and government accountability. The role of civil society in implementing those obligations is very important, and the future of the country's anti-corruption agenda depends on the involvement of civil society as much as possible in this matter, as well as ensuring that technical capacity, financial resources, access to information and open space to support and monitor it politically. The World Bank believes corruption is "the only obstacle to sustainable development and eradicating poverty."

According to Anti-Corruption Resource Centre: Dominant policy responses in anti-corruption still generally reflect the notion that corrupt practices are opportunistic and one-off. Most corruption risk management tools, for example, encourage the listing of potential individual acts of corruption to estimate their frequency. Yet, such an approach may not be appropriate for anti-corruption work in sectors where corruption is entrenched. Being sensitive to how corruption operates as a system is one way to arrest the endless inheritance of dysfunction, capture, fraud and misappropriation in certain important public areas.[44]

Conclusion

Corruption and its several forms, such as bribery, is one of the illnesses that paralyze the health of an economy. It is a big obstacle towards creating a sensible, equitable and sustainable economy. If it does not enjoy the administrative health of supervisory and support institutions, any economic system will suffer from such illness, and its functioning will be disrupted. Problems such as bribery are among the diseases that can paralyze the process of economic transition. The stronger and more resistant the economic foundation is to various events, the fewer societal problems will have. Usually, every coherent economic system, although it claims to organize production, distribution, and consumption in the form of its own ideas and intellectual foundations, any case, destructive factors also threaten it and damages its mechanism. The most serious aspect of corruption is when it becomes a cultural phenomenon. In this case, widespread corruption fuels political instability as citizens are willing to overthrow corrupt leaders and those who do not defend the public interest.

Chapter 19 -
Spiritual solution to economic problems

Introduction

It is the general understanding of people that religion deals with moral and spiritual aspects of life and economics with the material side. Knowing this, what has religion to do with economic life? If we look at the typical economics textbooks, the answer from the economists' viewpoint is obvious: nothing. However, in recent years, several economists have shown concern and interest in the relationship between economics and religion. The subject has attracted the interest of academic institutions and business organisations. Other terms used for this discipline include spiritual economics, divine economy, eco-spirituality, and ethical economics. Business ethics is an important area of the economics of business.

Economics and spirituality are partners

This chapter aims to show that moral, spiritual, and economics are partners, not enemies, and should go hand in hand. Issues such as poverty, inequality, and wealth are characteristics of the subject of economics. On the other hand, spirituality addresses issues such as love, compassion, caring and sacrifice. From this point of view, spirituality and economics are two separate subjects. They each have a different task to perform. However, by means of mutual coordination and collaboration between material and spiritual undertakings, significant progress is made in advancing the high goals of humanity and the development and progress of the whole society.

Looking at some of the reasons for economic problems, such as corruption, excessive consumerism, lack of justice in banking institutions, lack of proper management in the distribution of natural resources, relentless competition, mismanagement of government budgets, and incorrect policies related to misuse of government property, this chapter will conclude that a significant amount of economic problems we are facing today should be dealt with moral and spiritual principles and not limited to political and economic solutions only.

It was a culture shock for us living in one of the poorest countries in the world, Bangladesh, and then to two of the world's wealthiest nations, Canada and the UK. The conditions of living disorder, disparity, and extreme wealth and poverty I witnessed among these nations were not sensible, equitable, and sustainable. It needed to be addressed and explored by examining its causes and symptoms. In this part, without denouncing the role of capital investment, technology, and innovations, an alternative remedy to reduce the pain and frustration of poverty will be discussed: managing the societal lifestyle with the spiritual solution to economic problems.

Most people relate the subject of economics with phrases such as prices, supply and demand, finance, wages, cost and expenditures, goods and services and similar items. This view, however, is a narrow understanding of economics. For this subject to become more sensitive and meaningful, we must redefine economics without rejecting the above phases. Economics is about the market participants. They maintain a relationship with each other through means such as prices, commodities, supply and demand, etc. Economic relationships must be based on moral and spiritual principles to become meaningful and acceptable. Therefore, in the following section, we will redefine the two keywords of spirituality and economics. We must redefine spirituality to comprise people, including those distanced from the phrase spirituality. And we need to redefine economics in a way that agrees with spirituality. The final analysis is that economics and spirituality are not enemies but are partners. Although each has a different role and meaning, together provide a unique and extraordinary outcome.

Redefining spirituality

To welcome the entire population to participate in creating purposeful globalisation, it is sensible to reconcile the viewpoints of social scientists, theologians, people of Faiths and secular thinkers in embracing and applying a common concept of spirituality. The following working definition of spirituality is suggested here to be used for a better understanding of the motives behind effective social justice: 'Spirituality is defined as the all-unifying agency for developing and interconnecting our life with the material world, other people, our natural environment, and the future generation; beyond human limitations.' Based on this definition and its features of unifying and relational aspects, an alternative interpretation of spirituality is possible for establishing economic justice. This definition not only contributes to the betterment of external social conditions such as poverty, inequality, population displacement, environmental destruction, and the material side of life but also the higher nature of human beings represented by qualities of justice and fairness. Justice and fairness are virtues that have their place in the higher nature of human beings and are sources of human perfection.

For spiritual solutions to economic problems to become more meaningful and all-encompassing, the above definition of spirituality is suggested in a way that comprises all. This includes those who, for various reasons, try to distance themselves from religion and consider themselves secular thinkers. In other words, they consider themselves spiritual but not affiliated with any organised religion. All holy scriptures believe that humans are gifted with a higher nature, but it needs to be nurtured and developed. The belief in the higher nature of human beings also closely correlates with the purpose of life for a believer. The purpose of life is not simply the satisfaction of one's own needs and enjoyment of material pleasures but also involves service to one's community and the wider society. David Hay, a professor of child psychology at Aberdeen University in Scotland, gives a similar interpretation of spirituality as a unifying factor. He states, "Secular thinkers and social scientists can recognise spirituality when facing problems."[45] Therefore, spirituality has a unifying function, and it doesn't matter what kind of belief we have; we recognise spiritual principles when facing problems.

Considering the above discussion on the concept of spirituality and economics, the mention of a few examples will be helpful:

• The global financial crisis of 2008 led to the recognition of spiritual principles. It is now believed that the root cause of the global economic problem was not money but the absence of honesty, trustworthiness, truthfulness, and mismanagement of funds in financial institutions. A one-dimensional solution adopted mainly through monetary instruments will not be sufficient and effective in dealing with numerous injustices resulting from the current market system.

• The European economic crisis led to recognising a need for political unity among member states. The European leaders coming face-to-face with the recent financial and political crisis led them to realise that the root cause of problems is not the Euro currency but the self-interest of member states, mismanagement of money, and absence of political unity among themselves.

• As social scientists come face-to-face with ecological problems, spiritual principles are recognised. The UN invited World leaders and gathered several times to consult about environmental issues. They agreed that international topics such as the environment require all nations to consult, cooperate, show respect, and care for the planet. They decided that this requires a great deal of moral and spiritual maturity.

• When the rich and developed countries faced the current surge of refugees, they started to show compassion and welcomed them to have a better life. They have realised a positive potential in refugees. With appropriate policies, this rich source of human capital can be harnessed with benefits for everyone.

• Coming face to face with the problem of poverty at the global level, rich people and nations have recognised the need to show compassion and caring to bring the poor out of poverty. As a result, absolute poverty has declined by five hundred million people in the past few decades, and according to the United Nations, it is expected to be eliminated by 2030, which is having a minimum standard of living including access to food, clothes, housing, health and education.

• The recent development caused by COVID-19 signals that we must see the world as one big family and that pain, suffering and restlessness in one part of the world also affect others. The current Pandemic required an urgent need for cooperation, solidarity, compassion, caring and sharing, and a service-orientated approach.

The problem today when envisioning spirituality is that no economic system emerged within a just governance or is populated primarily by spiritually motivated economic actors. These conditions, just governance and spiritually inspired economic actors appear to be prerequisites of a future 'spiritual economy'. We can distinguish three functional categories that constitute ways to study economics:

- individual behaviour
- institutional behaviour
- economic systems behaviour

We can find straightforward prescriptions for the first and second of these categories. The third one, the study of the way economic systems behave, is the most difficult to advance our understanding. No existing economic systems operate according to the 'reality' of just governance and motivated economic actors.

Redefining economics

Justice issues should be among the key factors when discussing contemporary economic principles. If economics is defined as the optimal use of resources and justice as giving to each one what they are due. In that case, the two principles of economics and justice are both functionally and morally partners. The term economy comes from the Greek word 'Oikonomia'. The origin of this word denotes 'household management' or a person skilled in this area who ensures the management of the house and the well-being of all members of a nation. Suppose the economy is a general organisation system arrangement in a broader society. In that case, the household can be compared to organisations, including governments, responsible for managing a nation's resources for the betterment of the entire population. Therefore, the role of government is to establish legislation to ensure the well-being and prosperity of the country. This symbolic example of the function of a household has direct relevance to the subject of distributive justice with the vital role of governments in creating a balanced economy through the transformation of consciousness and behaviour of people.

One of the basic assumptions of free-market capitalism is that market actors are rational thinkers, and the market reaches equilibrium by itself; hence, there is no need for government intervention. External shocks exposed some of the flaws of this way of thinking in free-market capitalism. It was partly due to government intervention that the lives of many were saved, or the virus did not continue for longer. The main motive of a capitalist is in areas that produce maximum profits and numerous activities in a society that do not generate profit.

One of the challenges of current globalisation facing humanity is the adverse and harmful 'evil' consequence of materialism. Examples of the evil of materialism with its social, moral, and economic repercussions include inequality, consumerism, damaging the natural environment, and various negative externalities that are destructive to human life. The observations of such challenges and their effects on people's lives are significant in understanding and redefining happiness and prosperity. The solution to prevailing economic difficulties is to be sought by applying spiritual principles in implementing scientific methods and approaches. Therefore, a one-dimensional resolution adopted mainly through monetary instruments would not be sufficient and effective in dealing with numerous injustices formed because of the current market outcomes.

Economic justice will be attained only when every member of society enjoys a relative degree of material prosperity and gives due regard to acquiring spiritual qualities. Therefore, a discussion of the duality of human nature would be helpful. This means the signs of material and spiritual existence are found in humans. The view is that the nature of human beings is altruistic and not egoistic. People who act to further the interests of others ultimately serve their interests. Human beings should strive to reach this level of thoughtfulness. The individual is not merely a self-interested economic unit aiming to claim an ever-greater share of the world's material resources. By consecrating oneself to the service of others, one finds meaning and purpose in life and contributes to the upliftment of society itself.

Applying spiritual solution

The basis of the spiritual solution to economic problems is that the relationship between different agents or actors of the market should be based on a partnership between material and spiritual guidelines. The idea is that it is only possible to know the actual behaviour of buyers and sellers through income and prices. The fundamental laws of supply and demand will only be effective once and when accompanied by moral and spiritual incentives such as the four principles of consultation, cooperation, compassion, and moderation, which are the pillars of this model.

Therefore, the basis of this model is that economics needs to be understood. Economics is about people, and when it goes wrong, people suffer. Economics is not about money and prices and products. It is about people who use resources to live and have a good life. It is about relationships between people in the market, and ethical principles play a vital role anytime we talk about relationships.

Volatile markets

The current economic systems that follow the democratic structure are often designed according to the free-market theory. In some communities, most policies are mandated and determined by the government, and in others, these systems operate in combination with each other on different scales. It is very straightforward if we want to examine the inefficiency of these systems. It is enough to glance at the societies around us and perceive and observe their problems and crises. The main problem with these economic systems is their basic assumptions about human nature. In these systems, humans are considered competitive, self-interested and materialistic. While in countless examples, it can be seen that people's self-interest cannot solve the problem, and people can overcome difficulties with their altruistic behaviour. For instance, in the crisis caused by the recent Pandemic of coronavirus, we observed global solidarity and interconnection; countless people overwhelmed this global crisis by becoming united. This incident shows that humans are naturally not competitive and self-seeking and can have cooperative and altruistic relationships. Additionally, humans depend on each other, and national borders cannot separate people. This way, dependency can be cut off.

Economic systems following such assumptions have caused massive crises around the world. First, due to their competitive and materialistic nature, they have started to consume more of the precious resources of this planet, the effects of which have been global warming, air pollution, the loss of life of other organisms, rising sea levels, and has reduced the welfare of the people of the world. It is essential to know that the economy is the driving force of many other components of society, such as the political and legal systems. Also, it is necessary to understand that the economy is the driving force of many other community members. People in high positions of authority and financial strength can influence political decisions and elections with a resulting winning power. This creates a vicious cycle on a large scale that concentrates power and wealth in only one place. That is, the people who have more wealth are the owners of power and politics, and the decisions they make for individuals are such that they include their benefit. This is the dominant truth in today's world, and this is why comfort and prosperity, which is the right of all people, have become the share of only a few people.

Conclusion

Economics and spirituality, as two independent but complementary systems, should be placed next to each other to spread equitability, sustainability, and prosperity. An economy without spirituality causes moral deterioration, loss of collective interests, poverty and inequality, corruption, environmental destruction, class domination, mismanagement of money in financial institutions and government budgetary system and much more. Also, spirituality needs an economy to respond to the requirements of human material life. Material achievements are not the ultimate goals but a means to create communities where justice leads to human well-being. Consequently, regardless of social class, everyone can overcome their material problems with their efforts, take advantage of the available resources and cultivate the material and spiritual aspects of their lives.

Therefore, to achieve such an important goal, people must review the presuppositions and concepts governing society and take effective measures in this direction.

Chapter 20 -
Is the time right for an international single currency?

History of a single currency

An international single currency is when all countries adopt a single currency or join themselves in a single currency. A regional currency is when several countries have a single currency, such as the Euro currency in the European Union.

The global financial crisis in 2008 and the Euro currency crisis may immediately raise a concern that introducing an international single currency may not be as promising as it appeared. By looking at the Eurozone's economic condition since 2008, the opponents of a single currency may argue that the idea of a single currency is not working. The United Kingdom government, for example, opposed European single currency and exited the European Union. Experts in the European Union advocate the regulation and readjustment of the financial market as a necessary condition for the stability of the market.

The argument is based on separating monetary[46] and fiscal[47] policies. This section argues that the disfunctioning of a single currency is not due to currency itself but to the management, administration, control and organisational skills of those operating it. The proposition is that having an international single currency benefits a global economy. The current economic imbalances resulting from currency fluctuations are not beneficial to any country and cannot continue forever. According to Joseph Stiglitz, "the current imbalances are fundamental structural problems with the global reserve system, [here Stiglitz refers to ideas of John Maynard Keynes of how to reform the global monetary system] including creating a new reserve system based on a new international currency, can, with a little work, be adapted to today's economy"[48] The problem of the global financial system, therefore, is systematic and has much to do with the global reserve system, which improves global stability in the financial market. Supporting Keynes's view about a new international currency, Stiglitz argues that "It would enhance global stability and global equity."[49]

One lesson learned from the 2008 global financial crisis is that due to increased capital mobility and economic interdependency, one financial crisis in one part of the world can have a devastating effect on other parts of the world. Following the crisis, we see more coordinated action between Central Banks, which will increase in the coming years, the reason for our economies' structure. According to international financial economists Charles Wyplosz and Richard Baldwin, in an Optimal Currency Area, where a group of countries are better off with a common currency than keeping separate national currencies, and also where there is labour and capital mobility, the single currency takes away the risk of exchange fluctuation and associated costs. Wyplosz and Baldwin write:

For the business community and private sector, taking the risk of our exchange out of their business cycle equation is advantageous. It also makes perfect sense where economies are converging and there is increased trading exchange. I suggest exploring some history of currency and its development; in the past, each town and region used to have their currency, so trade was always much more complicated. Currency is not the driver of the exchange but the vehicle to make the business more accessible and transparent.[50]

Wyplosz and Maldwin's idea is appropriate for a global economy where there is a need for transparency and more straightforward transaction. There is also unpredictability and volatility of exchange rates.

Favouring an international single currency, Morrison Bonpasse argues that using single money can eliminate such volatility:

Economists continue to try to understand why, when, and by how much exchange rates rise and fall, and a substantial portion of the published articles about the international monetary system are about those exchange rate fluctuations. However, there will always be a partial answer, which is why the system must be replaced with a Single Global Currency.[51]

Agreeing with Bonpasse, Joseph Stiglitz argued, "Economists might like to believe that economic forces underlie all prices, but the prices of national currencies, at least, are determined as much by politics as by economics."[52]

The global financial crisis of 2008 was universal and affected both developed and developing countries. Looking at the problem and relating it to the currency situation, Stiglitz wrote, "There is a straightforward solution, one which was recognised long ago by Keynes: the international community can provide a new form of fiat money to act as reserves (Keynes called his new money 'bancor')."[53] Stiglitz called them 'global greenbacks', similar to the Special Drawing Rights (SDR)[54] of the International Monetary

Fund (IMF). He wrote that the concept of global greenbacks "simply extends the concept' of SDRs and that global greenbacks would be issued annually, unlike SDRs, which are published episodically."[55]

One hundred eighty currencies are circulating in 197 United Nations member countries.[56] It is estimated that transaction costs related to currency exchanges are billions of dollars annually.[57] Such a transaction method would benefit certain groups, such as banks and other financial institutions, creating employment opportunities. Countries are constantly competing to promote their respective currencies on the global market, and currencies that become stronger are more valuable and consequently in higher demand. Governments intervene in the money markets at different times and resort to managed exchange rate systems to manipulate the exchange rate to gain an advantage over their competitors. Multinational corporations invest only in countries whose currencies are favourable to their operations; otherwise, they relocate their businesses elsewhere.

The creation of an international single currency cannot take place overnight. Many factors must be considered before one is chosen or created. The success of regional currencies such as the 'East Caribbean Dollar – XCD' and 'West African Franc –

CFA' are notable and have harmonised several nations' economies. These represent a positive movement and a good factor for forming an international currency. These regional currencies have provided an opportunity to further understand the nature of an international single currency. As a result, economists are now far better informed about what an international currency may involve.

International Single Currency and globalisation

In the 20th century, not only the discussion of the globalisation of affairs in economic, social, political, and environmental terms intensified between politicians and experts, but at the same time, problems in all fields became more complicated. Hundreds of international conferences are held annually to solve the problems, and until now, there has yet to be a fundamental solution that can be used. Since the establishment of the United Nations, the answer to the problem of poverty has been to transfer money from rich countries to developing countries. This solution did not only work but added to the problem because developing countries became dependent on wealthy nations and the United Nations for their resources.

Poverty and inequality are just two examples of dozens of globalisation-related issues. Today, the globalisation of affairs is not a fantasy but a fact that will happen whether we like it. It is strange that to solve economic problems, the plan to create a single world currency has been given less attention. Is it because the time has yet to come, or the necessary prerequisites for its operation have yet to be created? In an age where the dependence between nations is increasing in all fields, a global monetary unit system will be one of the measures that will solve many problems at all levels of society. We will analyse it further.

The monetary crises in many parts of the world, whose economies have been tough hit, have demonstrated the fragility of the international financial system. While some countries and regions have been insulated so far from the genuine economic hardship and dislocation caused by these crises, specialists in international finance have warned repeatedly that a possible effect would be that a deepening economic collapse in one region could spread elsewhere if not worldwide.

Such warnings stem from the fact, now well established, that the world's economy is entirely integrated today. While this integration offers a degree of redundancy and resiliency, it also calls for much greater attention to the whole system - and mandates greater cooperation to ensure the economy's proper functioning. Government leaders, economists, business leaders and others have raised the call to reform the global financial system. As policymakers consider the options, the long-neglected idea of establishing a world currency system deserves a thorough investigation.

The idea of a world currency has been introduced previously. Economist John Maynard Keynes proposed an "International Currency Union" in the 1940s. His concept was watered down at the Bretton Woods Conference by diplomats afraid of something quite so dramatic. In its place emerged the International Monetary Fund and the World Bank. More recently, The Economist, among the most orthodox financial journals, called for a re-examination of the idea, suggesting in a 26 September 1998 article that 'One world, one money' might be worth a moment's thought'. Supporting John Maynard Keynes' vision of an international currency, Joseph Stiglitz, an economist and Nobel Prize winner, argues that creating such a currency will strengthen economic stability and justice at the global level.

Under the present system, over a trillion dollars change hands daily as investors seek the best returns for the least risk. These currency movements are managed by professionals who must anticipate or protect themselves against adverse changes in exchange rates, which often leads to speculation for or against particular currencies. Governments frequently intervene to defend their currency's position or seek trade advantages. The system is fundamentally unjust since countries with money as a reserve currency receive undue economic benefits compared to less favoured countries' currencies.

On balance, the success of a single currency, whether at the regional or international level, depends on whether it can promote economic justice in the world. It also depends on whether, in an Optimal Currency Area, it removes the advantages enjoyed by a few favoured countries, whose currency is seen as strong or more secure than others and stops people experiencing poverty from being affected severely by the impact of currency fluctuations. In the long run, adopting an international single currency depends on whether it offsets the harm that economic globalisation may cause locally by putting everyone everywhere on a more level of the economic playing field. Hence, this teaching may become controversial if it is not devised and implemented correctly and does not stimulate economic justice.

Supporting arguments

An international single currency operating under a central bank has specific economic implications and advantages over the current system of 180 separate currencies in circulation worldwide. Advantages include:

• Among the factors that facilitate economic transactions globally is the benefit of giving independence, transparency, and responsibility to a central bank. It is generally believed that guaranteeing the central bank's independence from daily political pressures favours economic stability. It is also essential that the relevant institutions are accountable and transparent in what they do and how they do it. Transparency helps institutions and families correctly compare the prices of goods, services, and resources in the global market. This is necessary because of the distorting effect and volatility of the exchange rate, which may hinder trade. From an economic perspective, it is accepted that prices should act as a signalling factor for the optimal allocation of resources to improve economic efficiency. A single currency encourages more competition and efficiency because prices are more transparent. This should help increase efficiency because companies have to produce products that are sustainable and beneficial to humans and the environment to compete and stay in the market. If there is a single currency, the probability of this happening worldwide will be much higher.

- Another advantage of an international currency relates to the risks each currency creates for the other. It can be avoided by using a single currency. In the multi-dimensional currency market, countries constantly try to influence their currency to gain competitive influence. When the value of one currency is determined against another, all currencies are at stake. This can be one of the reasons for global economic inequality, instability, and unpredictability. In addition, multinational companies that have invested heavily in various countries risk losing their capital due to currency fluctuations. They transfer their business operations to countries with favourable conditions to avoid such losses. Such transfers cause severe economic problems for the host country, including more unemployment, less income for families, lower taxes for the government, and lower welfare levels for the people. Adopting a single global currency helps eliminate this significant risk and uncertainty from the economic equation.

- A single currency benefits the entire market, especially the private sector, by removing currency exchange risk from their business cycle equations. This model suits the global economy that needs transparency and simpler transactions. Economists are still trying to understand why, when, and by how much exchange rate increases and decreases are associated with exchange rate fluctuations. But there is never a completely satisfactory answer for it. Economic forces such as money supply and demand or conditions that are entirely out of control can be the leading cause of currency fluctuations. But the prices of national currency units, at least at the economic level, are determined to some extent by politics.

- The instability in exchange rates between currencies creates difficulties for international trade and investment, business planning, and national economies, impacting price fluctuations and leading to ups and downs in the economy. With any movement, there are winners and losers and general economic penalties. If a country opts for a fixed exchange rate, its monetary policy must defend that rate; if it chooses a managed float, it is open to speculative attacks. Central banks can intervene to protect their currency. Still, major currency crises today can quickly overwhelm national reserves and require international emergency assistance, which has amounted to tens of billions of dollars in recent years.

- The psychological dimension is essential in currency crises since much depends on investors' confidence in a particular currency. Yet trust is easily shaken and hard to restore. A world currency would eliminate the opportunity for speculation and provide universal assurance.

- An international single currency can be a regulatory factor for consumerism. Multiple factors make consumers spend more. One of them is the currency exchange rate between countries. People with a popular, valuable, or strong currency can buy imported products cheaper. This is because rich and developed countries with stronger currencies can import products at a more affordable price. The opposite is also true. Countries with weak currencies need help importing goods made by developed countries. The single global currency can play an essential role in improving this condition. A single currency, which has a single value in markets around the world, gives people in different countries the same purchasing power in trading with each other. A single global currency would eliminate the advantage of several countries with stronger or safer currencies. This prevents the effects of currency fluctuations from harming people experiencing poverty. This move will be an essential step in promoting economic justice.

- One of the problems of trading with other countries is that we can never predict in which direction the exchange rate will move. This kind of uncertainty can hinder fair trade, especially for smaller companies. The existence of a single global currency provides confidence and encourages business at all levels. It should be noted that small companies play an essential role in economic growth and development, including creating employment opportunities and the optimal use of economic resources.

- Since 1970, gold has been no longer the basis of money printing, but it depends on each country's Gross Domestic Product and economic growth. With a single global currency, developing countries are better positioned to increase their country's economic growth through long-term plans. Some long-term means to boost economic growth and development include education and training programs for necessary skills, technology, and advanced and appropriate technology. With a single currency, business organisations in developing countries can purchase machinery and modern technology from any country and produce products at the international standard level. Therefore, exports and imports take place without obstacles.

- An international single currency would also be an essential step in promoting economic justice in the world, removing the advantage of a few favoured countries whose currency is seen as stronger or more secure and preventing people with low incomes from being hurt by the impacts of currency fluctuations. In the long run, such a step would neutralise the local harm sometimes induced by economic globalisation by putting everyone, everywhere, on a more 'level economic playing field'. Consequently, an international single currency would eliminate the present problems of speculation, instability and uncertainty and provide a strong foundation for the growing world economy. It would reduce the high cost and risk of doing business internationally.

- A single currency imposes common economic challenges on all countries and forces them to face unpleasant realities. Various objections to a world currency have been raised in the past, ranging from the rational to the emotional. A single currency would impose everyday economic rigour on all countries and force them to face unpleasant realities. No longer could governments print money at will or ignore that they cannot live forever beyond their means. Yet, in many important ways, these would be positive developments.

Although a currency is essential in international fair trade, more is needed to improve living standards. Other factors such as availability of resources, employment opportunities, level of education, access to modern and advanced technology, consumer and producer trust, and price level are also important.

Opposing arguments

Despite the benefits of currency unification, there are problems related to how it is designed, managed, and regulated and the timing of its implementation. Therefore, it can be questioned in several ways, mainly economic policies:

- Assuming that the World Central Bank manages the global single currency, if the bank interest rate is based on the so-called 'one solution for all' policy, the set interest rate will be the same for all countries. In this case, there is a risk that the interest rate, which may be suitable for one country, may not be ideal for another. For example, countries with high inflation may require a higher interest rate.

- In comparison, countries with low economic growth or high unemployment may need a lower interest rate. In an ideal world with meaningful globalisation and sustainable development, where countries operate in a similar economic cycle, having the same interest rate would not be a problem. Individual governments can also coordinate their activities with their fiscal instruments to avoid conflict with World Bank policies and a single interest rate.

- A more significant proportion of the world's population lives in developing countries than in developed countries. In this case, changes in some economic policies, such as interest rates, may affect countries differently. Also, countries with high economic growth that may cause high inflation may require a higher bank interest, while countries with low economic growth or high unemployment may require a lower bank interest. Of course, in an ideal world with meaningful globalisation and sustainable development, where countries run the same economic cycle, having the same bank interest will not be a problem.

In the above two cases, individual governments can coordinate their activities with the financial instruments they have to avoid conflict with the World Bank policies and bank interest rates.

- Another fear is that abandoning national currencies and foreign exchange markets would increase unemployment in some regions because some occupations would become redundant. A more open and level economic 'playing field' would divert some jobs to other areas. But such transitions are occurring already - without any underlying sense of justice that a world currency with its levelling power entails.

- Another problem with the single currency relates to the adaptation of different countries to global crises that affect countries differently. For example, a sudden oil price change that affects the country that exports oil will have a different effect than the country that imports it. Economic imbalance often results from a need for coordination between countries in their policies for managing supply and demand. An ethical economy supports changing lifestyles and adopting the correct management attitude to create economic harmony. Many of the damages that economies face today have a global aspect. In the long run, adapting to such crises will often be better with the same coordinated policy between countries.

- Concerning the single currency, the cost arises from the possibility that the monetary policy is correct for the monetary union and may need to be corrected for individual countries. Of course, the experience of the European Union and other regions with a single currency shows that these countries have used it well when facing economic problems by relying more on the second tool, national fiscal policies that include taxes and government spending. Therefore, coordinating monetary and fiscal policies is the best way to stabilise the macroeconomy. The adoption of the single currency under the supervision of the World Central Bank will cause a lack of cooperation and coordination between the two monetary and fiscal systems.

- At the regional level, gains from adopting the Euro currency came at the cost of abandoning monetary policy as a stabilisation tool. Two experts in the European economy, Mike Artis and Fredrick Nixson, confirm this. According to them, "The monetary union entails the loss of one important tool of national macroeconomic stabilisation policy which would need to be compensated by greater reliance on a second such tool, namely national fiscal policies."[58] According to Artis and Nixson, the assessment of benefits and costs comes down to a few distinct considerations:

> Benefits come from gains for trade and growth and the elimination of exchange rate risk; costs stem from the possibility that the monetary policy right for the monetary union is wrong for the individual country. This cost could take the concrete form of greater volatility of inflation and growth without a monetary policy instrument to help absorb idiosyncratic shocks (shocks to an individual country that do not affect the currency union as a whole).[59]

The question that should be addressed is whether the failure of a single currency is because of the currency itself or because of the lack of managerial, administrative, control, and organisational skills of those who manage it.

Further considerations

A lesson learned from the global financial crisis of 2008 is that due to increased capital movement and economic interdependence, a financial crisis in one part of the world may have a devastating effect on other parts of the world. Of course, after the problem, we saw more coordinated actions between central banks, which will increase in the future, proving the economic structure at the global level. In the context of the optimal currency area, where a group of countries with a single currency are in a far better position than maintaining separate national currencies and where there is the movement of labour and capital, the single currency reduces the risk of currency fluctuations and associated costs. An example is the Euro currency. One of the challenges in creating the Euro currency is that during its design, other economic factors, such as the level of wages and taxes and the transfer of human resources in different countries and the entire region, needed to be optimally designed. And most importantly, a kind of political unity has yet to emerge in the area.

The strength and economic support of the countries lie in their human resource. Human resource causes economic growth and development and creates economic stability for a long time. A type of currency is only a means to measure the goals of economic growth. The most important capital of a country is its human resources. With a common currency, competing by manipulating national currencies is unnecessary. Instead, competition is through the optimal use of valuable resources at their disposal. Human resource is an active economic factor that causes the use of other resources, such as land and capital. There are many examples in this case that the proper use of human resources has increased economic growth and reduced poverty in the country. For instance, a country like Bangladesh, whose national currency is not recognised in international trade and does not have high demand, now has sustainable economic growth due to the great importance of human resources. Of course, economic growth differs in developed and developing countries, and the amount of money in circulation for economic activities varies for these two countries.

Adopting a world currency alone will only solve some of the world's problems. One element is needed to support a more just and effective world economic system. It is one feature of the world federal system necessary to accompany globalisation and achieve world unity and peace. Ultimately, technical solutions to economic problems will only work effectively if a new spirit permeates economic life and a new economic system is evolved based on applying spiritual principles. Money itself needs to be put back in its place as a medium of exchange rather than a measure of economic performance or development. Social and spiritual values must balance economic values.

For an international single currency to be successful, it needs some prerequisites. One of the necessary prerequisites is to create a type of education and training to acquire skills at the global level and include all workers in all countries. Workers with adaptable skills will be ready to reduce structural unemployment. Wages will also be balanced globally. Therefore, there is a need for a type of education system that is universal and compulsory.

Another prerequisite is that large business organisations use the principle of cooperation instead of aggressive competition. This allows small business organisations to stay in the market without fear. And just as large organisations benefit from the single currency, other organisations will also help. For example, an organisation has been formed in the European Union to prevent illegal and aggressive competition. At the global level, it is necessary to have an international regulatory organisation that makes decisions worldwide to keep everyone under control.

Whether regional or international, the success of a single currency depends on whether it can promote the two fundamental principles of trust and economic justice in the world. The principle of investors' trust in a particular currency is essential. Confidence is easily shaken and hard to restore. A single currency provides universal trust among market participants. It also depends on whether, in the region of the optimal monetary unit, it destroys the benefits enjoyed by the few countries that benefited from it, countries whose currency is stronger and less vulnerable than other currencies, and people with low incomes in those countries are less affected by exchange rate fluctuations. In the long run, adopting a single global currency depends on whether it compensates for the damage that economic globalisation may cause locally by putting everyone everywhere and with a more uniform economy. Therefore, if this idea needs to be appropriately designed and implemented and is not the driving force of economic justice, it may become a source of controversy.

A single world currency is a distant goal. Still, the logic behind it as a solution to some of the critical problems threatening our present economic well-being must be considered. Indeed, given the trends of global interdependence and integration, its desirability - and its ultimate inevitability - suggest that the idea should receive a thorough investigation by world leaders sooner rather than later.

Many other measures for integration, harmonisation and economic equilibrium must accompany it. It would require a solid and effective world monetary authority or central bank, working in the common interest and free from political manipulation, to manage the world currency, regulate the money supply, and ensure adequate liquidity without inflation. The creation of such an institution would go hand in hand with developing other mechanisms for global decision-making aimed at building trust and consensus among the world's governments.

The creation of a single international currency will take time to happen. Before choosing or creating, many necessary factors should be considered. The success of regional currencies such as the East Caribbean Dollar and the West African Franc is noteworthy, as they have harmonised the economies of several nations. These show a positive and promising movement towards forming a single global currency. These regional currencies have provided an opportunity to better understand the nature of the international currency. As a result, economists now have a much better understanding of what the international currency may entail and are better acquainted with its challenges.

Bank currency and Crypto currency

Can bank currency be replaced by Cryptocurrency? The standard definition of traditional, physical, and digital currency depends on how we store it. Digital currency, in particular, is a form of currency that is recorded and transferred through an online program. And we use the term cryptocurrency, which includes bitcoin and thousands of such currencies. The term digital currency is used for both bank currencies, such as credit cards and Cryptocurrency, such as bitcoin. Crypto stands for Cryptography.

The purpose of this part is not to encourage or discourage readers from participating in cryptocurrencies. Cryptocurrencies have recently entered the market and have advantages and disadvantages. In other words, they can have potential. Also, it is important to note that these currencies are not illegal and should be welcomed to be tested instead of banned or defeated. What matters is that participants do not go into it unthinkingly.

So far, cryptocurrencies have created excitement in the market. It has made some people successful, and others badly suffered. Those interested in cryptocurrency should get enough information and expertise before taking serious action. Cryptocurrencies fit into each situation differently, especially regarding security, trading, or investment strategy.

Regional currencies such as the euro and several others worldwide, as well as the emergence of the blockchain industry and cryptocurrency based on it, help to understand the challenges of a universal single currency and draw the attention of experts when the time comes for its implementation. Therefore, worries about bank currency and cryptocurrency should be viewed positively.

What is the purpose of cryptocurrency? What is the problem with bank currencies that cryptocurrency is supposed to answer? There is no doubt that there are many shortcomings in the organisation and management of the banking system. But will Cryptocurrency address these shortcomings at the individual and collective levels and in organisations that involve both the private and public sectors? Of course, it is too early to answer such a controversial issue, but it can be explained, examined and tested.

Since 2008, when we faced a severe economic crisis known as the global financial crisis, which was the most worrying time after the Great Depression of the 1930s, the whole market lost its trust and confidence. All those who thought that the leading cause of the 2008 economic crisis was money, including experts and policymakers, later realised that the reason was not money but the mismanagement of funds in the financial institutions. Therefore, people lost their trust in the banks, and the banks lost their faith in the people. Also, people lost their confidence in the governments, and governments lost their trust in the people, banks, and other commercial institutions. Therefore, the lack of faith in the market created a huge gap that had to be filled. The gap-filling was done in several ways. One is that governments have set strict rules and regulations for banks and large commercial organisations. These organisations are now controlled, regulated, and limited in size and activities. Another move was a cryptocurrency scheme and blockchain. Thus, the economic crisis created opportunities to fill the gaps in the monetary and financial markets.

Of course, cryptocurrencies experience much volatility because the market is new, and the volatility is very noticeable, especially vulnerable to the trading moves of giant traders. Giant capitalists (market whales) hold large amounts of a particular crypto. This means that the whole market can be vulnerable to the decisions of large investors.

Like any currency, cryptos will be practical and create balance and stability in the market if the participants in their transactions think and act logically, rationally, and ethically. The fact is that with bank currency, the market at different times and places were out of balance, and government intervention was required to make the market more stable. Of course, it also depends on every organisation, such as the public and private sectors and crypto producers, to think and act rationally and morally; otherwise, the whole system will fail, and there is much evidence for this.

Since cryptocurrency is not centralised, people with such currencies must operate outside legal banking networks to exchange them for bank currency. Such services are only available in some places, which concerns people with cryptos.

A point in favour of cryptocurrency is that if the proper and solid foundation for its creation and operation is laid, especially about the exit of intermediaries from the market, there is no doubt that in developing countries, economic resources will be used more efficiently and benefit all. This will bring prosperity to the people's lives, especially the farmers. Why can't governments do with the bank currency if cryptocurrencies can get these intermediaries out?

The authorities and financial institutions do not regulate the circulation of cryptocurrency exchanges in the market. Therefore, crypto owners do not enjoy the support of government agencies if a problem arises. Also, due to the lack of monitoring of the crypto market, it is impossible to return after trading. For example, if an error occurs, there is no government support, and no organisation can help fix a cryptocurrency mistake. Therefore, the growing popularity of cryptocurrency requires an immediate regulatory response. Currently, controlled and regulated digital currency exists in every country under a central bank and offers to create their banknotes digitally. Of course, there are many problems with common bank currency, mostly related to the performance and management of relevant organisations. The problem is with those who need to be more competent in effective banking or who find a political dimension and make decisions that lead to currency instability in the market. Therefore, instead of eliminating the bank's currencies, I recommend correcting the financial institutions in the right direction. In other words, cryptocurrency is a wake-up call for banks to reform themselves.

The role of central banks in the economy is vital. Central bank policy is the foundation of the global financial system. The responsibilities of central banks vary between countries, including ensuring macroeconomic stability. Central banks use a variety of tactics, mainly manipulating currency supply and interest rates for economic stability. For example, to create financial stability, a central bank may increase or decrease the amount of currency circulation to prevent inflation and recession. Therefore, cryptocurrency cannot eliminate central banks. But can they work side by side? The future will show.

The subject of confidence in cryptocurrency is debatable. In this industry, exchanges occur randomly, not through identifying the characters and identities of the owners. This system makes proper contracts with individuals or companies practically impossible, making trust less possible. But what does trust mean? Trust means that I produce what you expect of me, and I expect you to produce what is right for me. In economics, this type of activity is called the division of labour. Therefore, trust in society is related to making valuable goods and services for the people of a community. It means mutual trust based on both moral and economic principles.

Is cryptocurrency capable of building mutual trust in the division of labour? With cryptocurrency, do investors invest in areas that benefit society, or are activities based on self-interest? Does seeking one's interests agree with mutual trust? Is it possible to have trust and cooperation between small business organisations and giant multinational organisations? Is there trust or willingness among the rich people for voluntary redistribution of wealth? These are the questions that the cryptocurrency market participants need to respond to. The cryptocurrency market is new, and the future may have adequate answers to such questions.

Conclusion

The conclusion drawn from this discussion affirms that an international currency will benefit the global economy if it has a stable infrastructure with justice and fairness for the general public, as well as a means of creating unity among nations.

Justice and fairness do not apply to any means of transaction that do not have the three factors of economic freedom, equal opportunities and means of progress in society. The opposite of this view is also true; countries with these three factors have a lot of inspiration and high economic growth and development. It doesn't matter what currency they hold - any currency.

There is a kind of deprivation or gap in the market, and cryptocurrency is the answer to fill this gap. Such an idea has caused enthusiasm and eagerness among the people. Any delightful market condition that solves a problem becomes popular and increases demand. Excitement to win a competition, excitement to defeat corruption and excitement to create work. For some, it has been successful; for others, the excitement has passed quickly and even failed.

Undoubtedly, there has been a need for stronger and more popular currencies. Hence, in recent times, cryptocurrency has been created to fill this gap. Such an idea has caused enthusiasm and eagerness among the people. Any delightful market condition that solves a problem becomes popular and increases demand. Excitement to win a competition, excitement to defeat corruption and excitement to create work. For some, it has been successful; for others, the excitement has passed quickly and even failed.

The solution to our economic problems is neither bank currency nor modern digital currencies known as cryptocurrency but the need for decision-making by human capital based on economics and spiritual principles. Economics and spirituality are not enemies. They need to be reconciled and work together. Economics is defined superficially. Economics is not about prices and supply and demand. These are only the tools that are used. Economics speaks of the relationship between human beings, the relationship between buyers and sellers, the relationship between employers and employees, the relationship between bankers and borrowers, and the relationship between government and the people. And when it comes to the relationship between human beings, moral principles play an important role.

As for the future of cryptocurrency, the notion is that no one knows what its future will be, and even sceptics cannot deny that it does not seem to be going away any time soon.

Chapter 21 -
Social and economic consequences of discrimination

Introduction

Well-wishers and democratic governments have widely recognised discrimination of variance types in general and of minorities in particular and the restrictive regulations on their practices. It is also well-publicised by the media and documented by the United Nations Human Rights Commission. This chapter discusses the economic consequences of discrimination on the life of individuals, communities, businesses, and governments involved. The argument is that there is a strong correlation between discrimination and economic indicators such as employment and economic growth and development.

Discrimination harms the whole economy

There is a negative correlation between discrimination of any kind and employment opportunities. As discrimination increases, employment opportunity decreases. Unemployment severely affects individuals, businesses, communities, and the government. Its impact on individuals includes a low level of income, lack of savings, lower standard of living, poor health, and lack of incentive to work as an individual's know-how and proficiency become obsolete. In the long run, they may be categorised as discouraged workers. At the community level, discrimination leads to increasing unemployment and the consequences of lower economic growth and development and other interrelated and depressing social issues. Rising unemployment means less revenue for the government to spend, affecting public service quality. All types of discrimination make a government politically isolated, less prominent nationally and internationally and negatively affect its global trade.

The phenomenon of unemployment plays a devastating role in the moral and emotional foundations of the life of the unemployed. It fills the unemployed person with severe emotional pain and mental harm. Some research shows that the shocking statistics of suicides of people who have suffered from experiencing unemployment for a long time can be a suitable indicator for society's understanding of the inability to bear these victims of misfortune. The phenomenon of unemployment in the long term causes irreparable damage to the morale of the unemployed and the moral foundations of the whole society.

To identify and solve any problem, we must first find its root cause and check the reason for the rise of this problem. So, the first step to understanding the effects of unemployment is to find the causes of unemployment. One of the most critical issues that cause it is management problems. When enough resources are available but cannot be used properly and optimally, it is definitely caused by improper management of these resources, both materially and related to human resources. If the resources are used correctly and with proper management in advancing the development goals, we will never see capital accumulation, production will increase accordingly, human resources and other resources will be used optimally, and the business environment will be created properly.

Discrimination harms economic growth

Economic textbooks define economic growth as a percentage increase in a country's total output, measured by the Gross Domestic Product (GDP) method. The GDP is defined as the monetary value of all goods and services produced in a country, usually within one year.

On the one hand, there is a negative correlation between discrimination and GDP. This indicates that when discrimination is higher, GDP is lower. Various issues, including unemployment, lack of morale, lack of up-to-date training programs, and psychological, emotional and motivational factors on those discriminated, negatively affect a country's total output level, subsequently affecting economic growth negatively.

On the other hand, there is a positive correlation between respecting human rights and economic freedom, with socioeconomic development. Countries with good human rights records, freedom and equal opportunities for all citizens mean more people contribute to a country's economic performance, which means greater GDP and increasing economic growth.

In modern working practices, human resources are considered the most valuable asset of any organisation. Human resources constitute the ultimate basis for the wealth of nations. Capital and natural resources are passive factors of production; human beings are the active agents who accumulate capital, exploit natural resources, build social, economic and political organisations, and engage in development activities. Religious persecution is a significant barrier to developing human resources necessary for the growth and advancement of a community and a nation. Such government actions may cause young people to need more schooling and training to contribute to their community's progress and the country's development. It is disappointing that religious persecution has caused the loss of opportunities for members of the minorities, who are a creative, skilled and dedicated workforce. Investing more in education and training is an attractive opportunity directly impacting economic performance. Investment in education can increase the total supply of a capable labour force and improve the employment prospects of unemployed workers. The financial returns from extra investment in the education of religious minorities will be substantial if a country desires to benefit from international trade and achieve growth.

Responsibilities of a government

In an ideal, sensible, and equitable world, every human being as a citizen of society has rights that must be observed, and the government has the duty to protect them. These rights include the right to work, the right to life and life in society and security, which are intrinsically for everyone and provided by society. Throughout history, no significant institution has protected and monitored these rights. For example, if someone violated the rights of another person, his family members would take revenge on him with personal methods, and perhaps the revenge would lead to tribal wars and the death of thousands of guilty people. Therefore, with the development of nations and the emergence of a judicial institution, the laws passed for modern society. Hence, personal revenge disappears, and if a person violates the rights of another person, he will be prosecuted first by examining the evidence, a court will be held for him with just and competent judges, and according to the criminal law, which is one of the most important elements of every country where the types of crimes and appropriate punishments are written in it.

The obligations of a government, more specifically, are to protect the rights of all its citizens, provide security and protect the private property of all, raise the standard of living of people, a just redistribution of wealth in the country, adopt various measures for rapid economic growth and development, to adopt different methods to reduce unemployment, protecting workers and ensuring acceptable working conditions, using the resources of the country more effectively and efficiently, to provide equal opportunity for all citizens, to advance learning and science, to protect the more vulnerable communities, and raise the banner of justice in the country. A government distancing from these responsibilities misses the opportunity to serve the nation justly and honourably and, in many instances, becomes less prevalent within the country and internationally.

Religious discrimination

Unfortunately, religious discrimination and persecution are happening in many communities and even under the direction of governments. Religion is restricted, regulated, and discriminated against, and its members are persecuted worldwide. Brian J. Grim (2007) has identified four critical dimensions of how such restrictions are measured:

 i.   overall religious freedom
 ii. government favouritism of a limited number of religious groups
 iii. restrictive government regulation of religion
 iv. and social regulation of religion

According to his findings, a higher correlation is found in government ministerial regulation and lower levels with social law of religion. Grim believes that "while governments typically view religious regulation as necessary to maintain order and reduce potential violence, the irony is that more regulation leads to increased persecution, which means less order and more violence."[60] Government intervention by adopting the policy of religious persecution and economic exclusion of minorities can cause severe problems for the adherents of a Faith community in both the short term and the long term, and other interconnected complications for the entire economy. Countries with a policy of equal opportunity for all citizens have a better chance to benefit from its human resources for reducing unemployment and increasing economic growth and development.

Effects on unemployment

Unemployment is one of the biggest economic problems. This is the obvious and main reason for an unhealthy economic condition and the root of social and even political difficulties. Unemployment causes social crimes to increase, and it is also a factor in reducing social relations and making the individual's bond with the community discouraged. A society in which unemployment is on the rise and struggles with it quickly witnesses the decline of social flows such as compatibility, cooperation and advancement. The state of relations between the economic elements of a country can be measured by the phenomenon of unemployment, and as long as the unemployment rate exceeds a certain level, it is possible to understand the inappropriate functioning and inefficiency of various sectors of the economy of a country.

The systematic economic campaign against a minority causes high unemployment within the community and the whole nation. For members of the Bahá'í Faith that work done in a spirit of service is considered worship, becoming unemployed is not only a painful condition but also has an unpleasant bearing on one's economic, spiritual and emotional well-being.

There are several ways in which religious freedom and the absence of religious persecution could help increase economic growth by reducing unemployment. These include the morale and, hence, the productivity of the labour force in general and members of the minority. These effects could increase the demand for labour and reduce unemployment. It is also the case that religious freedom could protect specific jobs in which members of the religious minority specialise and are considered unique to a country's economy. For example, thousands of professionals in education, health and industry, who were members of religious minorities, left Iran after the Islamic Revolution of 1979. During this period, several organisations in both private and public sectors suffered due to a lack of skilled workforces.

Importance of religious freedom

Religious freedom generates incentives for members of minority groups to remain at work. It also inspires organisations to invest in human capital. The absence of religious persecution is one of the reasons that assure businesses that members of religious minorities will not leave the organisation. Hence companies are prepared to invest in improving members' skills and know-how. Investment in human resources would increase labour productivity, increase the quantity and quality of goods and services, and develop new products. The result would be more profit in the long run for the organisation and the improved well-being of the entire community. However, in countries with a policy of religious persecution, businesses do not show interest in investing in training programs for members of minority Faiths. There is no guarantee that employees from minority groups will continue staying in business. Simply, it is too risky to invest in members of minority Faiths. However, the situation varies from one organisation to another and depends on the attitude of employers and shareholders. Private companies recruit people from all Faiths to achieve business objectives without considering people's religious affiliations.

Costs of religious discrimination

There is an apparent sign of discrimination in such a climate with a lack of religious freedom and severe persecution. The economic expression of bias is that it results in an inefficient allocation of human resources and unfair wage differentials. Both public and private sectors may cause bias in the labour market based on one's Faith. In the public sector, it occurs through direct government intervention to ban the employment of members of minority Faiths. Discrimination in the private sector is different and is primarily due to prejudice. Also, it may be due to the risk of employing members of minority Faiths, or it may be too costly to recruit them because such employees are vulnerable to restrictive government regulations. Whatever the reason, some private businesses are refusing to employ members of minority Faiths.

Conclusion

In light of this perceived state of persecution of minorities and the failure of a government to provide religious freedom and equal opportunities for all its citizens, it can be concluded that discrimination and persecution as a means of religious regulation can lead to economic oppression and exclusion of the members of minority groups, which can have severe negative economic consequences for the entire nation. A government's duty is to recognise all its citizens' rights and freedoms. This should be stated in its constitution to guarantee that justice is maintained and will stop any oppression towards minorities.

Chapter 22 -
Economic impact of human rights

Introduction

The concept of human rights was introduced and led to the United Nations Charter of Human Rights, issued in 1948. This has been a powerful standard for the worldwide enforcement of various fundamental rights. In recent years the widespread concern about the violation of human rights has been very encouraging. With the Universal Declaration of Human Rights, people everywhere have realised the importance and value of human rights.

Observance of human rights is one of the most important issues that effectively reduces unemployment and increases a country's economic growth. In fact, respecting human rights creates suitable conditions for people to do business, invest and create employment. Respecting human rights attracts foreign and domestic investment, providing a suitable economic growth program. If human rights are respected in the country, people will work more safely and with more concentrate, increasing production and improving product quality. By observing human rights, people will easily find better working conditions and appropriate salaries in the labour market. This will reduce unemployment and increase social interaction. Valuing human rights increases public trust in the government and governance system. This will reduce the country's insecurity and instability, providing a suitable stand for economic growth. As a result, it can be said that the observance of human rights is one of the most important factors that influence the reduction of unemployment and increase the economic growth of a country.

The view of social rights

Social rights are rights that a person has as a member of society and have an impact on society with his or her personal and professional activity, such as the right to property, right to business, freedom of work and other social activities. In a broader sense, social rights refer to a series of laws that are known to the individual in order to eliminate social and economic injustices, and these injustices are caused by the economic and social conditions prevailing in the society and the environment in which the individual lives. As Pierre Bourdieu[61] writes: "Before being a citizen, a person is a farmer, a worker, a merchant, a doctor, etc." All these jobs and activities put a person in special and economic conditions in such a way that all kinds of pressures are directed at him. The requirements and pressures may be economic or social or, for example, discrimination which is possibly imposed on a group of minorities and on women, while freedom as a human right dictate that a person is free from such restrictions, discriminations and compulsions. Such injustices will be there unless the government undertakes positive obligations towards the individual, which are called social rights.

Social rights, like the rights and freedoms of a person, are the result of the requirements of human nature, which are as vital and fundamental for a person. Social rights go beyond the boundaries of individual rights and traditional freedoms and include a series of basic economic and social issues in society. Therefore, social rights in the general sense of the word include rights with economic content, such as the right to property, freedom of business and industry and commerce, which we study under the title of economic rights. The government has undertaken a series of positive commitments in advanced societies, such as providing work for everyone, improving workers' working and living conditions, social security, food, housing, welfare and health for all, which are very promising.

The purpose of economic rights is to regulate the system of private ownership of land and commercial and industrial establishments (tools of production) and to establish proper order in economic affairs, while the purpose of social rights is to regulate the relations of social life and work and to remove existing injustices.

Identification of social rights

During the Second World War, the goals that were stated for the first time by the heads of the victorious governments, and then stated in the Atlantic Charter as the goals of the United Nations, and then approved in the Yalta Conference held 4–11 February 1945, were emerged the provision of the four freedoms. They promised new things. These freedoms were: freedom of speech, freedom of religion, freedom from fear and freedom from need.

The United Nations considered these rights to be the first condition of social welfare and the basis of international peace and understanding, which constitute the content of social rights. The purpose of these rights is to free a person from all economic constraints and anxiety of any kind which destroys the dignity, personality, freedom and self-esteem.

Ensuring the material and economic independence of the individual and removing the fear and anxiety will make the individual live in a safe and secure environment in society and be able to benefit from other rights and freedoms in a favourable way, without which, of course, democracy would not be possible and will lose its meaning and concept.

Pierre Bourdieu consider several types of social rights, using the 1934 plan of the North American National Resource Planning Institute and the declaration of the 26th International Labor Confederation meeting held in Philadelphia in April 1944. He considers social rights to include the following:

- The right to have a useful and productive job.
- The right to social welfare.
- The right to freely choose work and occupation.
- The right to strike and the right to form a union.
- Regulating the private property system.

Policymakers should remember that the measure of 'Gross Domestic Product' (GDP) is merely a tool to achieve more important goals, not an end in itself. Undoubtedly, resorting to this measure has many benefits in measuring the state of countries, especially when it increases. More jobs will be created, wages will increase, and the country's overall budget will increase so that the government can redistribute more wealth in society. But the ultimate goal is to 'improve the quality of life' of the people, especially for the worst-off individuals and families.

A positive correlation exists between respecting human rights, economic freedom and socioeconomic development. For example, providing more freedom and opportunities for members of minority groups and also for women to work and contribute to the economy means greater GDP and, hence increasing economic growth. The persecution of religious minorities and restrictive government regulations for women to participate freely in economic activities are obvious barriers to the nation's economic development.

Chapter 23 -
Promoting humanitarian and
philanthropic activities

Introduction

In modern times, the importance of humanitarian and philanthropic activities is recognized by communities. To make communities a better place for everyone, we all need to play our part in whatever way we can. Humanitarian and Philanthropic activities are an effective way. It can be of many forms, such as through voluntary services, offering our skills and professional ability to those who need our help, contributing to a charity organisation, setting up a social enterprise, and much more. The synonyms words are benevolent, altruistic, noble, generosity, gift, donation, charity, good-hearted, sharing and giving.

For those of us who would like to see a significant human transformation of the world, it is essential to ask whether one can practice economics in a moral, ethical and spiritual vacuum. The answer is no longer. Currently, a significant revolution in value systems is taking place, and its foundation has been led by civil society, like Non-Governmental Organisations, spiritual and religious movements and by the leaders in business and academia. As Alfredo Sfeir-Younis (2001) puts the key to this revolution is the move towards the humanisation of welfare economics, including philanthropic activities. He says: "Too much attention has been paid to the 'human doing', the 'human having' and the 'human knowing' and much less to the 'human being'. While 'having', 'doing' and 'knowing' is extremely important, the intrinsic value, direction and identity of human life (like solidarity, caring, sharing) are given by and are like the 'being'."

While we like to believe we can make a difference on our own, sometimes we can do more together, for example, by donating to a charity organisation. Helping others is an object close to the hearts of every human being. Contributing to the causes we care about benefits not only those who are receiving but also can be deeply rewarding for those donating. Thus, humanitarian and philanthropic activities are gratifying and life-changing for all involved. From the earliest times, society could only function by us working together. Selfless acts of looking after those who need it the most and the urge to help those around us are always inside us. So, giving is an important cause we care about and is a natural drive to help others. More affluent people should step forward and voluntarily take responsibility for improving the world.

The human behaviours of compassion and generosity are examples of virtues required for effective voluntary sharing. This approach is highly effective because it is done freely as a matter of choice rather than being forced to give. Reflecting upon this, it would appear that the spiritual laws of prosperity deal with receiving and giving helps. Whether this is because, in the future, humanity will become morally more conscious or the government regulations will become more effective for creating a better world by applying distributive justice. Even now, there is greater material prosperity in those countries with effective regulation of wealth redistribution.

On the one hand, the wealthier care for people experiencing poverty. On the other hand, those experiencing poverty should not force the rich to share their wealth. The balance is that the rich should extend assistance to those experiencing a modest standard of living but of their own free will, not because they have gained this end by force. Yet, this may become a challenge for both groups. It can be challenging for the rich to voluntarily share a portion of their wealth with those unknown. Also, it is difficult for people with low incomes not to expect or try to gain this by force. The process leading to distributive justice morally requires much trust in the system. Morally speaking, it is also essential to how wealth is created. Morally, the first condition for acquiring wealth is that one's efforts must earn it. This confirms the need to work and be a productive community member. The second condition is the income spent on charitable and philanthropic activities. This indicates that people are engaged towards attaining a culture of philanthropic, humanitarian and benevolent activities.

Altruistic nature of human beings

People are altruistic and willing to transfer some of their wealth to those worse off than themselves. Altruism is said to exist when one individual's well-being contains elements of both the individual's well-being and that of others. This benevolent act improves their standard of living. The fact that many charity organisations are helping to improve the lives of people experiencing poverty supports such altruistic nature of human beings. We remember the experience of COVID-19, which brought people closer to each other through benevolent and selfless actions.

Although the vast responsibility of caring for those experiencing poverty is left to the rich, the rich should voluntarily and compassionately carry out this responsibility for the well-being and happiness of others because they have more economic resources at their disposal. The benevolent behaviours of compassion and generosity are examples of virtues necessary for effective voluntary sharing. This action is considered very effective because giving is based on the individual's choice and not by force. Although the responsibility of the rich to care for those experiencing poverty is well-known, the burden of others should not be ignored, such as the government and business organisations. It is a combination of factors that should be considered to correct unpleasant economic conditions and related symptoms.

The redistribution of income and wealth is determined based on factors such as income level, ability, inheritance, education, market structure and charitable actions. We can argue that if everyone lives in a single society with the same distribution of income, then the result is simple and understandable, in the sense that each caring person will benefit from another caring person helping people experiencing poverty, and therefore each will have a chance to benefit from it. But we don't live in such conditions. Thus, at the government level, the redistribution of income and wealth is done with multiple policies. For example, taxes are used to pay for public expenditures. The tax system can be adjusted so that wealthier people share more costs. A significant part of public expenditure includes benefits paid to people in need from government aid through subsidies.

Voluntary giving and the goal of unity

The relationship between the voluntary redistribution of wealth and the goal of unity is worth some reflection. There is a direct relationship between unity and voluntary and benevolent giving. Acquiring wealth is acceptable to the extent that it is used to achieve higher ends. The ultimate goal for every person should be reaching the unity of humankind. For example, how can we enjoy our wealth while millions of people worldwide live in absolute poverty? Today, many rich disposes of their wealth by forcing them to pay taxes and try to avoid them as much as possible. However, for their happiness, the rich will be forced to spend their wealth to provide better conditions for the society in which they live. Therefore, the view is that in the future, when people will enjoy more spiritual advancements and become aware of the needs of others, then the effects of wealth in society will be understood, and charitable actions will be done with a foundation of goodwill and joy.

Many reasons can motivate us to provide and support a particular form of humanitarian and benevolent activities. Currently, there are different solutions in terms of applying the benevolent principle. While we like to believe that we can make a difference and make the world a better place, sometimes we can do more together, for example, by donating to a charity organisation that can improve the lives of many needy people. Donating to causes we care about can benefit those who receive it and ourselves. Altruism exists when one person's well-being has elements of others' well-being. This benevolent action improves their living standards. At the same time, benevolent actions give a person a sense of happiness and inner satisfaction. Spending for ourselves can be satisfying, but spending to help others brings joy and peace of mind.

Sharing xperiences with family members

Human societies have always been able to work and progress with cooperation. Self-sacrifice to care for those who need it most and the desire to help those around us have always been and is within us. Therefore, generosity is a natural motivation to help others. The act of giving creates and revives the feeling of social conscience. For many people, having the ability to improve the lives of others is a privilege that comes with a sense of obligation. Acting on these powerful feelings of responsibility is a great way to reinforce our values and feel like we are living in a way that aligns with our beliefs. With charitable donations, we remind friends and family members, especially children, that we care about them and want to support them. Children's participation at a young age can also help them feel responsible. Family giving creates bonds, helps strengthen relationships through a common goal, and often raises more donations than would otherwise be possible through individual contributions.

Sharing the experience of charitable donations with our children can create positive changes in their society and beyond in the world from an early age. Children naturally like to help others, so nurturing their innate generosity is likely to mean they grow up more appreciative of what they have and will continue to support charities and good causes in the years to come. Therefore, parents can be good role models for children. Children learn through what they live, especially in the family. Accordingly, parents can set a good example. Children learn what they live, so they are much more likely to grow up with caring and sympathetic attitudes when they see parents donating.

COVID-19 has encouraged many to look at their local communities and consider how they can make a difference. Humanitarian and Philanthropic actions such as helping charities, especially locally, can be a powerful way to invest in people and society. Donating a small part of our wealth to charity brings us closer to the community we want to live in and creates an ideal world. Imagine a society where no child goes hungry or is abused, no animal is harmed, all diseases are treatable or curable, and everyone is treated kindly and fairly with equal opportunities in life. This is what we are all collectively working towards. Real change requires action, but it cannot be done alone. Our voluntary contributions help charitable organisations to create a society that benefits everyone. For example, hundreds of social and economic development projects worldwide have improved millions of people's living conditions.

Risks of voluntary donations

However, in analysing the principle of voluntary giving of one's possession, the system may jeopardise the importance of several public services such as education, health and security. This will be too risky. This principle also can be challenged based on several other issues. Voluntary donation may not necessarily eliminate poverty. The reason is that such donations may provide a basis for some people never to work and may create a culture of dependency. Also, the financial aspects of a community, nation, and world cannot be built on a system based only on voluntary giving. A government cannot plan its public finances on such unpredictable sources of revenue.

Therefore, the process adopted through taxation is more practical in the wider society, though it may be better. As it is commonly practised in the wider society, the method of distributive justice is mainly through government intervention with regulatory bodies for using taxation and different types of subsidies. The effectiveness, however, depends on how the corruption and misuse of financial resources in public or private sectors affect a country or how distributive justice affects the economic growth of a nation.

Another argument against voluntary giving is that instincts drive humans to survive and satisfy their base desires. Hence, there is no simple correlation between economic growth and voluntary giving. For example, if we focus on selfishness, the idea of voluntary giving appears as a mirage, impractical and unrealistic. Also, voluntary giving in the form of charity often targets the symptoms rather than the cause of a problem and may only temporarily remedy issues such as eradicating poverty.

Conclusion

Humanitarian and Philanthropic activities and altruism through caring and sharing give us a sense of belonging. Life can be challenging at times, but we are all in this together in a community, and principles of benevolent activities can help us feel more connected to those around us. Therefore, by voluntarily assisting people in need, we can feel more that we are an active part of our society. This practice also helps a lot to strengthen self-confidence and self-esteem. Often, people in the community who are most in need are overlooked; therefore, voluntary participation and humanitarian actions help bridge the gaps and provide dedicated human and physical resources to help the most vulnerable.

Index

Notes and References

[1] https://devinit.org/resources/poverty-trends-global-regional-and-national/#:~:text=In%202021%20an%20estimated%20698,live%20below%20%245.50%20a%20day.

[2] Throughout this book, it is useful to distinguish between transitional economies and economics in transition. Transitional economies mainly refer to countries that transitioned their economy from socialism to capitalism, from a command economy to more free market economies. It is also about those countries that moved from agriculture to more industrial production. However, economics in transition for a better world is a general term that refers to the transformation of some aspect of the economy from now to the future, from today to tomorrow, and from the current state of the world to a better future.

[3] Report from the UN Commission on Environment and Development (Brundtland Commission),1987.

[4] Shapoor Rasekh. Shapour Rassekh, a distinguished professor of sociology at the University of Tehran before the 1979 Islamic Revolution, a pioneer of quantitative surveying in the country, a UNESCO consultant and author of numbers books and articles on sociology, economics and education.

[5] Adam Smith, the author of *The Wealth of Nations* (1776), is a Scottish philosopher and economist and is one of the principal founders of the classical economic system. Smith is the founder of microeconomics. It is about the market agents, including buyers and sellers, trading through supply and demand and a price system. The assumption is that the market automatically reaches equilibrium or a balance position, so minimum government intervention is needed.

[6] Karl Marx is the author of *'The Communist Manifesto (*1848) and is a philosopher and economist. The writings of Marx are

mostly about capitalism, which was dominant in the western world. Many experts believe that Marx's ideas can be an answer if capitalism must be reformed. Marx is the founder of the planned or commanded economic system, which means full government participation in economic activities.

[7] John Maynard Keynes is the author of *'The General Theory of Employment, Interest and Money (*1936) and is a British economist. Keynes, without discarding the microeconomics of Adam Smith, thought that for a national or global economy, microeconomics is not sufficient, it is not working effectively for a bigger economy, and therefore he introduced components of macroeconomics dealing with issues such as unemployment, inflation, economic growth, and factors affecting international trade. Keynes believed that the active participation of government is necessary to achieve these macroeconomic objectives.

[8] https://www.bruegel.org/blog-post/global-imbalances

[9] Suheil Bushrui. Quoted in Badee. Economics and the Bahá'í Faith, 2018, p. 213.

[10] Olupona, Jacob. (2009:xvi). *Spirituality in Africa*, *HARVARDgazette,* (http://news.harvard.edu/gazette/story/2015/10/the-spirituality-of-africa/)

[11] See Noris, P. and Inglehart, R. *Sacred and Secular: Religion and Politics Worldwide,* 2011.

[12] Stiglitz, Joseph. *Making Globalisation Work*, London: Penguin Books, 2006 p. 269.

[13] The Tiger Economies refers to countries which undergo rapid economic growth, usually accompanied by an increase in the standard of living. The term is used for the Asian Tigers, including South Korea, Thailand, Singapore, Malaysia, and Indonesia.

[14] BRIC is a grouping acronym which refers to the countries of Brazil, Russia, India, and China, deemed to be developing countries at a similar stage of newly advanced economic development, on their way to becoming developed countries.

[15] Farhad Rassekh and John Speir. *Journal of Global Ethics*, 2010, p. 27.

[16] Augusto Lopez-Claros and Daniel Perell. Future: Shaping its Agenda— Part I: Poverty, Inequality and Global Finance. April 24, 2023

[17] Universal House of Justice. Statement dated 1 March 2017.

[18] Farzam Arbab. Development - A Challenge to Bahá'í Scholars', *Bahá'í Studies Review*, 1984, pp. 1-18.

[19] Views presented by peace analyst Hussain Danish.

[20] Ervin Laszlo was an active member of the Club of Rome. The publication of the Limits to Growth (1972) raised interest in Laszlo's work, especially his club of Rome report, Goals for Mankind (1977)

[21] Aurelio Peccei and Alexander King.

[22] See Promise of World Peace, a statement by the Bahá'í world governing Body, the Universal House of Justice.

[23] Augusto Lopez-Claros and Daniel Perell. Future: Shaping its Agenda— Part I: Poverty, Inequality and Global Finance. April 24, 2023

[24] Universal House of Justice, *The promise of World Peace*, pp.1-2.

[25] Jeffrey Sachs is one of the advisers of the former Secretary of the United Nations, Kofi Annan.

[26] Jeffrey Sachs. The End of Poverty, Penguin Books, England, 2005, p. 12.

[27]<http://www.worldbank.org/en/news/press-release/2015/10/04/world-bank-forecasts-global-poverty-to-fall-below-10-for-first-time-major-hurdles-remain-in-goal-to-end-poverty-by-2030>

[28] The Perry Project was conducted from 1962–1967, but led to a longitudinal documentary as we continue to follow the Perry Preschool participants throughout their lives in this landmark study that forever changed the trajectory of early education. The Perry Preschool Project established the lasting human and financial value of early childhood education and led to the establishment of the High Scope Education Research Foundation and one of the first early childhood programs in the United States intentionally designed to increase school success for preschool children living in poverty.

https://highscope.org/perry-preschool-project/

[29] Smith, Adam. *The Wealth of Nations*, Tom Griffith (ed.), London: Wordsworth, 2012, p. 709.

[30] Ibid.

[31] Ibid.

[32] Utilitarians also expressed that we all should be in the greatest happiness. Jeremy Bentham and John Stuart Mill are the most eminent thinkers of this view. Utilitarians argued that to achieve 'the greatest happiness for the most significant number of people, income must be transferred from the rich to the poor up to complete equality, to the point at which there are no rich and no poor. According to utilitarianism, the reasoning is that everyone has the exact needs and the same capacity to enjoy life. See *The Oxford Dictionary of Philosophy*, p. 377.

[33] Massimo Motta. *Competition Policy: Theory and Practice*, Cambridge: Cambridge University Press, 2004, pp. 12-13. (In some countries like the UK, monopolies are regulated and monitored under Competition Commission (CC). Monopoly is defined as a firm having more than 25% market share. CC also make recommendations such as seeking changes in the firms' business practices, imposing price controls and even divestment. This introduces the possibility of structural interventions, which is more typical of regulatory regimes than competition policy.)

[34] Diseconomies of scale is when a business expands so much that the costs per unit increases.

[35] Michael Todaro. *Economic Development*, pp. 79-80. (Rostow wrote in the opening chapter of the stages of economic growth: the traditional society, the pre-conditions for take-off into self-sustaining growth, the take-off, the drive to maturity, and the age of the mass consumption.)

[36] <https://www.goodreads.com/quotes/80461-excellence-is-never-an-accident-it-is-always-the-result>

[37] Adam Smith. *The Wealth of Nations*, Tom Griffith (ed.), London: Wordsworth, 2012, p. 709.

[38] Ibid. *Theory of Moral Sentiments,* p. 83.

[39] John Maynard Keynes.

[40] Michael Parkin. *Economics*, 9th ed., London, Pearson Education, 2001, p. 5.

[41] Amartya Sen is Thomas W. Lamont University Professor, and Professor of Economics and Philosophy, at Harvard University and was until 2004 the Master of Trinity College, Cambridge. He is also Senior Fellow at the Harvard Society of Fellows. Earlier on he was Professor of Economics at Jadavpur University Calcutta, the Delhi School of Economics, and the London School of Economics, and Drummond Professor of Political Economy at Oxford University. and the Nobel Prize in Economics. See: https://scholar.harvard.edu/sen/biocv

[42] Cited in Jean-Pierre Mean. On corruption and bribery: fighting to restore trust, publication of European Bahá'í Business Forum, 2009, p. 7.

[43] Ibid. pp. 7-9.

[44] See: https://www.u4.no/blog/corruption-entrenched-systemic-resilient-anti-corruption-can-help

[45] David Hay. *Something There: The Biology of The Human Spirit*, London: Darton - Longman, 2006, p. 28.

[46] Monetary instruments include interest rate, exchange rate and money supply.

[47] Fiscal policy include government policies on taxation and spending.

[48] Ibid.

[49] Ibid. p. 268.

[50] Charles Wyplosz and Richard Maldwin. *The economics of European Integration*, London: McGraw – Hill Education, 2004, p. 16.

[51] Morrison Bonpasse. *The Single Global Currency*, p. 418.

[52] Joseph Stiglitz. *Making Globalisation work*, p. 259.

[53] Ibid. p. 260.

[54] The SDR is an international reserve asset created by the IMF in 1969 to supplement its member countries' official reserves.

[55] Joseph Stiglitz. *Making Globalisation work*, p. 261.

[56] <https://www.google.com/search?q=total+number+of+currenc ies+in+the+world&rlz=1C5CHFA_enGB985GB985&oq=total+ number+of+currencies+in+the+world&gs_lcrp=EgZjaHJvbWU

yBggAEEUYOdIBCTE1NTQ0ajBqN6gCALACAA&sourceid=
chrome&ie=UTF-8>

[57] Morrison Bonpasse. *The Single Global Currency*. p. 33.

[58] Artis and Nixson. *The Economics of the European Union*, p. 283.

[59] Ibid. p. 394.

[60] See B.J. Grim and R. Finke, "Religious Persecution in Cross-National Context: Clashing Civilizations or Regulated Economies?" *American Sociological Review* 72 (2007): 654.

[61] Pierre Bourdieu (1930 – 2002) was a French sociologist and public intellectual who was primarily concerned with the dynamics of power in society. His work on the sociology of culture continues to be highly influential, including his theories of social stratification that deals with status and power. Bourdieu was concerned with the nature of culture, how it is reproduced and transformed, how it connects to social stratification and the reproduction and exercise of power. One of his key contributions was the relationship between different types of such capital, including economic, cultural, social, and symbolic. Bourdieu's (1986) conceptualization of social capital is based on the recognition that capital is not only economic and that social exchanges are not purely self-interested and need to encompass 'capital and profit in all their forms'
See: https://www.socialcapitalresearch.com/bourdieu-on-social-capital-theory-of-capital/.

Milton Keynes UK
Ingram Content Group UK Ltd.
UKHW051050161123
432674UK00010B/72